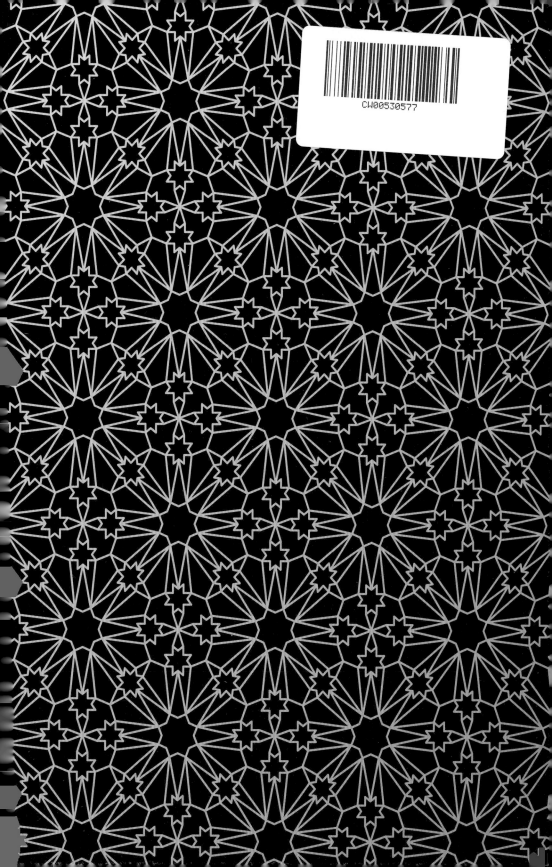

GENEROUS SOULS

Revealing the lives of the pious

VOLUME 1

Dr Muzamil Khan

In the name of God, the Most Compassionate,
the Most Merciful.

The 19 pious souls included in this volume are:

- Abu Sa'id Abi Al-Khayr ﷺ
- Hassan Mu'adib ﷺ
- Imam Nawawi ﷺ
- Miran Bhikh ﷺ
- Sultan Bahu ﷺ
- Sayyid Isa Gilani ﷺ
- Hafiz Muhammad Hayat ﷺ
- Sidi Bel Abbas ﷺ
- Sain Tawakkul Shah ﷺ
- Diwan Ali ﷺ

- Dhul Nun Al-Misri ﷺ
- Mawlana Ya'qub Charkhi ﷺ
- Beshir Osman Beshir ﷺ
- Hassan Al-Basri ﷺ
- Salih Al-Jafari ﷺ
- Javad Nurbakhsh ﷺ
- Shukri Al-Luhafi ﷺ
- Nizamuddin Awliya ﷺ
- Sayyidah Maymunah ﷺ

DEDICATION

I lovingly dedicate this book to Sultan Al-Arifin Bayazid Al-Bastami (804–874). He is a great source of inspiration for me. I visited his shrine in 1993 and 2007.

ACKNOWLEDGEMENTS

I would like to express my gratitude to the following individuals: the 'Ten', Eman, Cameron (Editor), Zubair, Yasin and Hannah (Designer).

CONTENTS

The best speech is from God, and the best guidance is from the Prophet ﷺ. After that, the best type of advice and counsel is from the pious people known as the *awliya* (saints). This book, *Generous Souls: Revealing the lives of the pious* is about individuals that are spread around the world – of diverse races, languages, eras and from both genders. However, they share a common thread and specific characteristics which, for the perceptive reader, are recognisable.

These traits are described in the Holy Qur'an – such as faith and piety – and in the Prophet's ﷺ words: *"When you look upon their faces, they remind you of God."* Various other traditions highlight some of their features. For example, they lack an elevated social status. They may appear needy or disadvantaged, to the extent that they are not esteemed by many. However, these pious people are very dear to God and were they to ask Him for something, He would surely grant it to them.

The lives of the *awliya* have been a passionate interest of mine since childhood. Throughout life, I have gained immense pleasure, guidance and help from their wisdom. I have written several books inspired by this love. I teach classes to young men and women, using the works of the *awliya* to help me convey their message. There is a saying that, *"I have a love for these pious people, although I am not one of them."* There is also some good news in the tradition of the Prophet ﷺ : *"You shall be with the one you love."* And so, I hope that I am with the pious people here and in the Hereafter.

This book is a selection of accounts about the *awliya* from my classes between 1993 and 2020 that I taught to young men (some of whom are now into their forties). I taught these classes using Arabic, Persian, Urdu, Punjabi and English texts. Apart from benefiting me personally, the stories of the *awliya* have been a guiding light and a source of blessing, clarity and comfort for the students.

All the classes were recorded and then transcribed, with transcripts running into thousands of pages. They were also summarised into articles by various people and printed for the benefit of the public whenever we celebrated that person's life.

In this first volume, I have focused on nineteen spiritual sages and nineteen different themes. The subsequent three volumes to follow will contain a further seventeen, eighteen and nineteen articles respectively. I feel this is my calling as I have always spent my energies in this field. I hope that, if God is pleased with this effort, that He includes me amongst these pious people we love. I wish to make their lives accessible to people who know little or nothing about them. In my view, this is an excellent service because these people led lives worth living, knowing and emulating.

The Watchful

EGO

Abu Sa'id Abi Al-Khayr (967–1049)

Abu Sa'id is one of the most famous Sufi saints of Iran. He was a Shafi'i scholar and a renowned poet. The two major works that deal with his life and teachings have come down to us in Persian. I have great personal admiration for him and often quote him in my lessons. This article was originally written as a summary by Syed Sajid and Majid in 2010.

Abu Sa'id was born in Meyhana in the province of Khorasan, northeast Iran. His father was called Abul Khayr - a chemist by profession, a Sufi and a lover of the awliya. Abu Sa'id's father was a great admirer of Sultan Mahmud Ghaznavi (971–1030). So, when he came to build a new house, he decorated all the walls with various images of the sultan. Abu Sa'id was only a child at the time, so he asked his father for a room of his own, which he began decorating by writing the word 'Allah' everywhere. When his father saw this, he asked why he had done this. Abu Sa'id replied, *"O father, you put the name of someone you admire, and I put the name of the One I love."*

Later, after he had begun his studies within the sciences with various renowned teachers, Abu Sa'id related his childhood meeting with the great Shaykh Abul Qasim Bishr:

"When I was learning the Holy Qur'an as a young boy, I went with my father to offer the Friday prayer. On the way, we had the blessed opportunity to meet the old Shaykh Abul Qasim. My father was a devotee of Shaykh Abul Qasim, who told him: "I do not want to leave this position empty after my demise. I am looking for someone to take over from me. However, no one seems capable of this responsibility. After seeing your son, I now have hope. After the prayer, bring him to me. God willing, a lot of benefit will come through him.""

"After the prayer, my father took me back to Shaykh Abul Qasim. We sat in his room, in which there was a tall cupboard. Shaykh Abul Qasim asked my father to place me onto his shoulders to reach the highest shelf and bring down a piece of bread. My father picked me up, and, as soon as I touched the bread, it became warm. Upon seeing this, Shaykh Abul Qasim broke the bread into two and began to cry. He handed one piece to me and kept the other. My father asked, "O Shaykh, forgive my bad manners, but I would like to share this blessing." Shaykh Abul Qasim replied, "I put that bread on top of that shelf thirty years ago and have been waiting for this sign; for someone whose touch would make the bread warm. That is the person whose destiny it is to carry on my responsibility. It is your son who has this share, and this cannot be divided. No other can carry the spirituality which is in your son's destiny. O Abul Khayr, you must look after this child; from him, much benefit will come to the world." Shaykh Abul Qasim then turned to me and said, "Not for one moment should you divert your attention from God. This is better for you than everything on which the sun sets." He then asked me if I desired to speak with God, to which I replied that I wanted nothing more. He then gave me a couplet to recite in seclusion, saying: "Keep reading this, and you will get to speak with Him.""

> Be tu jana qarar natavanm kard
> Ishsan tu ra shumar natavanm kard

> Without you, O Beloved, I am unable to rest,
> Your favours I cannot assess.

Gar bar tan-e man zaban shavad har mu'e
Yek shukr tu az hazar natavanm kard

If every hair on my body became a tongue,
A thousandth of gratitude to You, I cannot express.

I kept reading this until God opened my heart, and I began to understand Divine mysteries."

Following this meeting with Shaykh Abul Qasim, Abu Sa'id was blessed to understand Divine mysteries not usually expected of a young boy. The following incident demonstrates the depth of understanding he had attained. One day, Abu Sa'id was instructed by his mother to accompany his father. At the same time, he attended a sama – a gathering where poetry was recited without music. That evening, the following poem was recited at the end of the ceremony:

God gives the darwishes love, and love is war
By dying near to Him, they grow
The generous youth will freely yield his life
The man of God cares not for worldly show

Aurally, this poem had an immense impact on the young Abu Sa'id, so he enquired from his father what it meant – what message it proclaimed. His father informed him, *"It is just poetry. It has no significant meaning."*

However, even at such a tender age, Abu Sa'id was blessed with great mystical insight. He realised that there must be a conscious purpose encoded within this fragment of poetry, and thus he memorised it. Later on, he would narrate: *"What I understood from this couplet was that the whole purpose of Sufism is to unite us with our Creator."*

The couplet explains the universal truth that we are all in love with ourselves. What is hugely beneficial to us is to love someone other than ourselves, such as our masters. If you fall in love with your shaykh, then the ego will gradually, but inevitably, die; hence, we can die before dying, so to speak. The ego is a barrier that keeps us from connecting with God. The only way of reaching Him is to let go of ourselves, as nobody can reach Him with their egos intact. As Shaykh Tamastani states: *"The greatest blessing is to escape from the ego because the ego is the greatest veil between you and God."*

In all religions and all societies, some individuals attempt to control their egos. Even though their existence is worldly, they set out to avert the desires which attend to their earthly lives, even at the expense of any success in worldly terms. Many religions create complex traditions of self-control. They believe that by doing this, they gain control of their ego.

However, within Islam – a *din* (religion) of moderation – the process to overcome the ego differs. This guidance teaches us to purify the heart by ridding it of its desires. Because, as God says, *"God has not made for any man two hearts in his (one) body"* (33:4). Therefore the awliya continuously strive to attain the ego's subjection, ensuring they have just one heart - a heart turned fully towards God. The prevailing ideology is that we must begin by trying to understand and know Him, if we desire to reach Him. However, it is not so simple.

"You wish to know God while your ego exists, but your ego does not even know itself; how can it know another?" – Hakim Tirmidhi (820–869)

Even knowledge of our physical body is limited, as we are often obliged to visit a doctor for our medical problems. Likewise, we also remain unaware that every part of our physical body is under the ego's influence. It uses our senses for its purpose: like the eyes that become a source of temptation through what they see and crave. Likewise, the tongue becomes devious by its utterances. In brief, we begin to worship our ego through our senses. *"Have you seen the one whose god is his ego?"* (25:43). Ego-worship is the most dangerous deviation from pure faith - it is, in fact, hidden idolatry. A person could do many good deeds in their life, and then, in a flash, their ego could swoop in and wipe away everything.

Hence, it must be confronted in this life; otherwise, darkness will obscure the soul, the light of every action. The ego's most devastating effect may show itself when the person in question has still not gained closeness to God after a lifetime of righteousness.

Considering this, Abu Hafs Haddad (d.879) warns that a seeker must suspect his ego at every moment, even though it may continuously try to assure that it will not oppose. This is the practice of the *awliya* - they begin by understanding the ego and becoming aware of its trickery. They are aware that if a person tries to progress but has not controlled and subdued their ego, he will slip at the most critical time, just as the devil did.

Shaykh Kharaqani (963–1033) comments, *"There are two things of which I have not reached the end. One is the station of the Prophet ﷺ ; the other is the deception of the ego."* The ego's deception is such that a person is never aware of the guise in which it will attack. It is like a chameleon changing every moment, putting up a smokescreen to confuse the individual between the real and the fake. However, suppose the ego's trickery is understood. In that case, people can still train themselves to see what stems from the ego and what does not.

Our masters explained how difficult it is to spot the ego - they say finding it is like noticing a black ant, on a black rock, on a moonless night. Baba Farid (1173-1265) narrates, *"One day, I asked my master, Shaykh Qutbuddin (1173–1235), for permission to go into seclusion. He replied by saying there was no need to do so as it could bring about unwanted fame. I informed my master my intention was pure, and I was not trying to attract attention but, on the contrary, to control my ego. My master remained quiet. At that very moment, I thought about what I had just done. I was trying to suppress my ego, and in doing so, I had just contradicted my shaykh. I never forgave myself, and for the rest of my life, I always thought, why did I answer back?"*

We will continuously be tricked by it, but to think for one moment that we can completely slip its betrayal is also a thought that stems from the ego. Therefore, those people who are aware of its tricks use every moment as an opportunity to correct themselves. A person cannot attempt to oppose or challenge their ego directly, for it will devour them. The *awliya* advise us not to provoke the ego but to negotiate with it. Imam Busiri said, *"The ego is like a child; you do not stop it from doing things. You gradually wean it off."* Suppose, for example, it says it wants to do something sinful. In that case, a person should begin to negotiate with it by offering something it will still enjoy but is less harmful. One should not provoke it by doing a holy act, as this will only be a means to more significant harm down the line. Therefore, the *awliya* teach people not to challenge but to wean the ego from what it wants. Above all, you must be tactful.

At this point, it should be clear that to even think about tackling the ego unaided is suicide. So, the question becomes, what is the key? What is the easiest method of emptying the heart of the desires of the ego? When someone wants to learn a skill or trade, they approach a master in that skill. And so, in this case, the masters to approach are the awliya. A follower should reflect that he cannot understand his shaykh, though he often meets him. So how can he hope to understand the Prophet ﷺ and God? This insight into a devotee's thoughts will increase the strength of his connection with his shaykh and help kindle such a feeling of love.

Love is of exceptional quality. Once a devotee loves his shaykh, this affection will be the source of all goodness. That person will only have to make a minimal effort in physical terms. Still, a tremendous amount of progress will occur to aid that person in transcending their ego. This is because love for the shaykh fills a person's heart and gradually flushes out any negativity within their soul. Due to this love, the devotee's heart connects with the pure heart of his shaykh. From this connection, the shaykh will gradually, in small doses, begin to cleanse the person's heart of various selfish characteristics.

Still merely a young boy, Abu Sa'id studied the science of *Hadith* and met numerous awliya but was yet to meet his master. However, events soon unfolded, which would ultimately lead him to meet with his shaykh. Once, on his way home from school, Abu Sa'id was noticed by a baker, who asked about the books he was carrying. *"What book are you reading?"* he said. Abu Sa'id mentioned the book, and the baker replied to him, *"Real knowledge is what is hidden; you cannot attain it all through books."*

Abu Sa'id later noted, *"At this stage, I did not understand what he was saying. I was under the impression that I would get all the knowledge from my books. He was saying there is knowledge beyond the books."* What seemed like an insignificant event became the catalyst for an extraordinary change in his life. Following this, he met a mystic, Luqman, who introduced him to his real master - his guide on the spiritual path. Abu Sa'id narrates: *"In the eyes of the people, Luqman was crazy, as he would deter people through his strange and erratic behaviour. One day I passed the rubbish heap, and, as usual, Luqman was sitting in the middle of the filth and dirt. When he saw me, he picked up some filth and was about to throw it at me. I opened my chest and said, 'welcome'. When he saw that I did not react as any other child would have, he took me by the hand and led me into the presence of Shaykh Abul Fadl, who later became my master."* Luqman had tested the patience of Abu Sa'id. He immediately understood that Abu Sa'id had not reacted according to the wishes of his ego. Luqman took Abu Sa'id to Shaykh Abul Fadl, who became his master.

In their meeting, Shaykh Abul Fadl said to Abu Sa'id: *"Abu Sa'id, one-hundred and twenty-four thousand prophets have come and told people to come to God. Those people who connected with this message from the prophets began remembering their Lord. Gradually, His name, which was on their tongues, became imprinted on their hearts, and no longer needed to be repeated by the tongue."* Shaykh Abul Fadl's words had an immense impact on Abu Sa'id, such that he became restless and could not sleep at night. He thought to himself constantly: *"How do I reach that stage at which my heart will remember God and experience what my Shaykh told me?"*

The next morning, Abu Sa'id went to see his teacher, Shaykh Abu Ali Faqih, who explained the verse - *"Say 'Allah' and leave them to amuse themselves in their folly."* (6:91). Shaykh Abu Ali explained that when the heart is awake with God's remembrance, God will command them to say His name and leave others. Listening to this verse, Abu Sa'id understood that this was exactly the message Shaykh Abul Fadl had given him the previous day - to say 'Allah' and leave people to their situations. He suddenly fell into a trance. At that moment, he felt a door to his heart had opened. Upon noticing this, Shaykh Abu Ali asked, *"O Abu Sa'id, where were you the day before?"* To which Abu Sa'id replied, *"With Shaykh Abul Fadl". Shaykh Abu Ali then advised him, "Return to your master immediately, as your condition requires his focus."*

Abu Sa'id then returned to Shaykh Abul Fadl, who told him to repeat 'Allah' with his tongue until it imprinted on his heart. When the heart is clean, a person can see the ego approaching before it can attack. Shaykh Abul Fadl used the technique of *'dhikr al-qalb'* (the heart's remembrance) as a method to help Abu Sa'id achieve this. By following this teaching, Abu Sa'id felt the presence of God in his whole being. Soon after this, he went into seclusion.

One day Shaykh Abul Fadl said to Abu Sa'id, *"The time has come for you to return to your village. There you will be granted an opening."* This instruction from Shaykh Abul Fadl was the sign for Abu Sa'id to complete his spiritual training - his heart now related to God. This was the indication from his shaykh that God's command had arrived. Abu Sa'id was to begin his spiritual work trying to bring about change in the hearts of others. Abu Sa'id then followed his shaykh's instruction and received many blessings.

Later, after his master died, Abu Sa'id still felt in need of guidance. Hence, he visited Shaykh Abul Abbas Qassab and spent much time in his company. We have seen how the men of God spend their lives under God's Will by learning how to subdue the ego. However, many of them may still feel that they have not taken complete control of themselves. For this reason, they keep a very watchful eye over the ego. Although such men may be saints, they need the guidance of their masters to further develop their faith.

A shaykh once ordered his devotee to visit Shaykh Bayazid Al-Bastami (804-874) before he departed for *Hajj*. After a long and arduous journey, the devotee arrived at Bastam. He ate and rested, and then he met Shaykh Bayazid, who asked him, *"What does your shaykh teach you?"* The devotee replied, *"O Master, my shaykh teaches us, 'When you receive, give thanks, and when you don't, be patient.'"* Shaykh Bayazid smiled and said, *"The dogs of Bastam do no different."* Shocked by such a response, he blurted out, *"So what is it that you teach?"* Shaykh Bayazid replied, *"When we receive, we give away, and when we don't, we give thanks."* After this, the devotee decided to delay his *Hajj* and instead return to his shaykh. He mentioned what had happened, and the shaykh went into a trance. Afterwards, he told the devotee to return to Bastam and ask Shaykh Bayazid for advice. The devotee obeyed and returned to Bastam. He asked Shaykh Bayazid, *"O Master, my shaykh has sent me to ask you for some advice."* Shaykh Bayazid angrily picked up a blank piece of paper and scrunched it up before throwing it to the floor. Completely baffled by this response, the devotee returned to his master. *"So what did Shaykh Bayazid say?"* he asked. *"He did not say anything,"* replied the devotee. The shaykh said that this was totally impossible and that Shaykh Bayazid must have done something. At this point, the devotee showed him the piece of paper. The shaykh suddenly went into ecstasy. He later explained to the confused devotee: *"My son, Shaykh Bayazid, taught me to let go of everything - to become like that blank piece of paper."* Soon after this incident, the shaykh died. Later it was revealed that he was stuck in a spiritual state. Through Shaykh Bayazid's guidance, he overcame this hurdle and eventually reached a lofty spiritual rank.

The *awliya* can distinguish the different types of egos and see a person's true nature immediately. They see a particular defect and then immediately begin to rectify the disease. The cure could appear in various forms, but the seeker must always possess certain qualities for its effects to work. In many discussions, Abu Sa'id would describe the qualities required to be free from the ego. He explains: *"No less than the ten characteristics which I mention must be present in a sincere disciple if he is to be worthy of discipleship."*

If a person has these ten noble qualities, he may one day control his personal dragon - the ego. He must first be intelligent enough to understand his shaykh's indications. He must then be obedient to carry out his command. He must be sharp of hearing to perceive what his shaykh is saying. He must have an enlightened heart to see the greatness of his master. He must be truthful so that whatever he may report, he reports it accurately. He must be true to his word and keep every promise he makes. He must be generous. He must be discreet so that he can keep a secret. He must be receptive to the wisdom of others to accept his master's advice. Finally, he must be chivalrous; he needs to be prepared to sacrifice his own life for the mystic path.

> *"Know that opposing the ego is the beginning of worship."*
> – Imam Qushayri (986–1074)

However, before opposing the ego, you must first become aware of the variety of traits it displays. Naturally, these are countless, but the ego's most common characteristic is that it dislikes change. Change tends to mean that you are trying to move it from its preferred, settled position. The ego loves to give orders but hates to obey, as it is also very lazy. It uses your own intellect to confuse you. Allama Iqbal explains that intellect in itself is devious. It can change its colour like a chameleon, but true love never changes. The ego is envious and will never offer praise to others. Instead, it will try to belittle anyone it perceives as a threat. It is not willing to let go of hatred, and thus it uses anger as its fuel. It wears so many faces that, in the end, the individual will never actually know who he really is. A shaykh knows which of these areas the ego is coming from. It is a different area for everybody, so the shaykh will prescribe a different treatment process. A look or even a handshake from the shaykh may show he is quietly working on a person's ego, burning away some of its evil traits.

Being a master himself, Abu Sa'id constantly worked on the state of his devotees. It is quickly noticeable from examples of his teachings that no two egos he observed were the same. Each person required a different cure, hence the difficulty and delicateness required in correcting people. The same dose of medicine cannot be administered to everyone, and the same goes for correcting the ego. Abu Sa'id implicitly knew each person's capacity, along with what they each required from him to help them work on themselves. Therefore, his teaching method covered various techniques, but 'sama' was his predominant procedure.

When Abu Sa'id started the practice of sama within Nishapur, he quickly faced opposition. Soon enough, his enemies complained to Sultan Mahmud Ghaznavi. The sultan replied to the people that they were free to take whatever actions they deemed necessary. The people took this as a pass to kill Abu Sa'id and his devotees. Understandably, this frightened all the followers of sama, but none dared to speak directly to Abu Sa'id about their apprehensions.

On the other hand, Abu Sa'id himself did not show the slightest concern. Instead, he called Hassan and said, *"For breakfast, serve everyone boiled lamb heads, plenty of sugar, plenty of sweets and rosewater. Moreover, burn some incense and set all the food on clean white cotton cloth in the middle of the city mosque, so those who talk behind our backs can see that God's Hand feeds from the unseen."*

Although Hassan did not have the means to arrange a meal for one hundred and twenty people at the lodge, he made his way to the market. He pondered whether to beg or return and mentioned to the shaykh that he had no provisions to purchase the food. He decided to stay, and he expected something would happen to take care of matters. The market closed, and it became dark, but still, he remained waiting. Suddenly, a man approached Hassan and asked him, *"What are you doing here? There are no shops open."* After listening to Hassan, the man smiled, opened a bag, and said, *"Take as much money as you need."* The following morning, the people were bewildered to see that the shaykh and his followers enjoyed a lavish breakfast in the city centre. Angered by what they saw. They sent a message to the tribal leader Abu Bakr Ishaq, who responded, *"Let them enjoy their last meal, tomorrow vultures will eat them."* After this miraculous breakfast, Abu Sa'id said to Hassan, *"Go and prepare the front row at the mosque for Friday prayer for all the devotees."*

The imam of the mosque, Mufti Sa'id, was one of the people who opposed Abu Sa'id. Following the prayers, Mufti Sa'id engaged himself in a lengthy supplication, and Abu Sa'id stood to leave. Mufti Sa'id stared at Abu Sa'id, implying it was bad manners for him to leave while he was still busy supplicating. Abu Sa'id, in return, gave him a look that rendered him powerless. He felt as though he was a pigeon in the presence of a hawk. Following this exchange of glances, Mufti Sa'id's opinion changed. He no longer wanted to be part of any group that desired to cause harm.

After leaving the mosque, Abu Sa'id said to Hassan, *"Go and get some pastries and take them to Abu Bakr Ishaq. Invite him to join us in the evening so that he may break his fast with us."* Abu Bakr Ishaq was surprised by the message, for he had not informed anyone about his optional fast. He was also perplexed by the gift of pastries because before the Friday prayers, he had walked past a shop and desired the exact same pastries. Realising that this was no mere coincidence, Abu Bakr's opinion of the shaykh also changed. So he sent a message to those people who opposed the shaykh, announcing, *"I am not going to cooperate with you in your plans to martyr the shaykh and his followers."* Abu Bakr Ishaq continued, *"Say to your master that Sultan Mahmud, with one-hundred thousand men and seven-hundred war elephants, could not defeat us. However, your pastries have won us over. We are now your servants."*

Hassan related the message back to Abu Sa'id, who explained: *"Since yesterday, you have been shaking from fear, terrified at being hung for being a Sufi. It takes someone of the calibre of Mansur Al-Hallaj (858–922) to be hanged - real men are hanged, not impostors."* He then asked the *qawwal* to recite the following poem describing a 'real' Darwish:

> *To the battlefield, come prepared*
> *With an array of thought of self just follow us*
> *Whether life is like the water of fire, live happily*
> *Amid it be content.*

One day, Abu Sa'id went to the *hammam* (public baths) and commented to Abu Muhammad, a close friend, *"This hammam is a pleasant place. Why do you think this is so?"* Abu Muhammad replied, *"O Shaykh, it is because of your presence - this is what makes it a blessed place."* Abu Sa'id replied, *"No, this is not the real reason. This is a pleasant place. All you need to remove the dirt is a jug of water and a towel, and even those do not belong to you."*

Here, Abu Sa'id explained the virtue of keeping yourself light, just like a person newly born into this world, free from possessions. Like a light-traveller moving from one place to another, we should live lives of very little means, as we too are travelling. Indeed, we must learn to live free from possessions. This was how Abu Sa'id lived his life; he was a master at recognising the ego and its trickery.

One day, Abu Sa'id attended a gathering in a different village. The announcer wanted to describe the full backstory of the eminent shaykh to the people gathered. Although he had asked the master's devotees about Abu Sa'id, the announcer was still unsatisfied and wanted to know more. Abu Sa'id noticed all this and said to the announcer, *"Say, nobody, son of nobody."*

"Until you become an unbeliever in yourself, you cannot become a believer in God."

Abu Sa'id

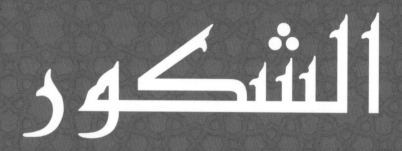

The Most Appreciative

SERVICE

Hassan Mu'adib

Hassan was neither a scholar nor a Sufi master. His fame rests on his role as the personal assistant of Shaykh Abu Sa'id. In my view, his life and service are worthy of merit. Indeed, one of my aims throughout my teachings has been to introduce neglected personalities like Hassan to my students. I believe we can greatly benefit from the example of his dedication to his master and his family. The article was compiled in 2012 by Afdal and Saheed.

'He who serves will one day be served.'

Abu Sa'id never claimed to be anything. He really did refer to himself as 'nobody, son of nobody'. Later described as 'the Master who lived his life in finding his own faults', he was proficient in dealing with the trickery and mischief of the lower self - 'the ego'. Once, he advised a devotee: *"My message can be written on a fingernail. The summary of all my teachings is to sacrifice your ego."*

It so happened that a young man from a noble and wealthy family was intrigued by Shaykh Abu Sa'id. He was sceptical of his ability to read people's thoughts - especially since he did not believe that God had even revealed this knowledge to His Prophet ﷺ. Confident of his intelligence and wit, he sought out Shaykh Abu Sa'id at a gathering with the sole intention of testing him. When he entered the gathering, he sat quietly and patiently among the devotees to avoid attention.

From the comfort of his distant position, he could see the shaykh, who was delivering a sermon. Afterwards, Shaykh Abu Sa'id pointed towards a poor man and requested the audience to donate some of their clothes to him. All present offered something to the poor man, except for this young man. He was dressed in the most elegant attire, wearing conspicuously expensive garments; he was certainly in no mood to part with them. He remained seated and unmoved by the charitable atmosphere. One of Shaykh Abu Sa'id's devotees then approached him and requested that he donate his turban to the poor man. He had now found himself in a predicament. He had come to test the shaykh, but now he was being coerced in turn into giving up his expensive turban. The young man retorted: *"This turban is worth ten dinars and, furthermore, it was a gift."* He stubbornly refused to part with his turban.

Shaykh Abu Sa'id noticed his reluctance and intervened: *"Young man, give your turban to this poor man."* He still could not part with his turban. Then an old man who had witnessed all this asked Shaykh Abu Sa'id: *"O master, does God ever speak to His servants?"* Shaykh Abu Sa'id replied: *"Yes, He does, and He will not ask more than twice for an expensive turban. He has asked the man sitting by your side twice. However, he is more concerned about the monetary value of the turban."* Shaykh Abu Sa'id's words caused the young man to tremble, and he immediately fell at the shaykh's feet. His heart was emptied of all disapproval and hostility towards the shaykh. He removed his expensive turban and his outer garments and gave them all to the poor man. From this point onwards, he became devoted to following Shaykh Abu Sa'id and would sacrifice all his wealth and time for the sake of the shaykh. His name was Hassan, and Shaykh Abu Sa'id gave him the title of Mu'adib, which meant a person with good manners.

Indeed, his good manners were his defining virtue throughout his time with the shaykh. They were pivotal in him receiving the honorific title of *'Khadim-e Khas'* (Personal Assistant). In that first request to sacrifice his expensive turban for another person's benefit, Hassan was implicitly taught the importance of service to others. It is this characteristic of dutiful servitude that he had learned in his first meeting with the shaykh.

There are times when a small act of service offered sincerely can prove better than many deeds of worship. During a campaign under the sweltering heat, the Prophet ﷺ had his Companions camp at a suitable location. Some were fasting while others were not. Due to exhaustion, those who were fasting soon fell asleep. The others carried water for those who set up tents to shade the whole company. When the time arrived to break the fast, the Prophet ﷺ said: *"Those who did not fast today have received rewards greater than those who did."*

Despite his Companions' protests, the Prophet ﷺ himself carried stones on his back during Quba and the Prophet's mosque. The exceptional modesty and true spirit embodied by the Prophet ﷺ are a unique example for all Muslims. Indeed, his entire life was one unrelenting act of service to God and creation. Had this not been the case, as Imam-e Rabbani (1564–1624) emphasises, the Prophet ﷺ would not have been referred to as the 'abd ('Servant') in the testimony of faith. As a pre-requisite, each Muslim is required to repeat this testimony - further proof that this honour must be the pinnacle of achievements in God's sight. Had there been a worthier honour, then surely the Prophet ﷺ would have received it. Thus, the road to acquiring eternity lies in serving others with a genuine heart. Subsequently, service has immense importance in Sufi training.

Khwaja Ubaydullah Ahrar (1404–1490) ascribes his own spiritual level to the blessings of his service. He states, *"We have not covered the distance on this path solely from reading books on Sufism. But by putting into practice what we read and serving the public. Each is provided with a certain path, and we were liberated through the path of service."* This shows that knowledge alone is not enough without putting what is learned into practice through the act of service. Yet, Divine acceptance of a particular form of service given depends on its bearing certain qualities. An accepted or 'ideal' service, in this sense, would be to seek the pleasure of the Lord by approaching creation with a sincere, compassionate, and selfless heart. In other words, serving must not be marred by self-interest in any way. It must instead be offered genuinely, with the only rewards in mind being those of the Hereafter.

Shaykh Abu Sa'id was aware, of course, that Hassan was not without his faults, but he saw potential in him. So he began to delicately remedy his flaws. Hassan had a certain sense of arrogance due to his noble background. If he was to succeed in becoming an excellent servant, then, indeed, such an unavoidable flaw must be washed away. On one occasion, Shaykh Abu Sa'id instructed Hassan to go to the marketplace to purchase tripe and then carry it through the market on his back. He did as instructed and soon found himself walking through the marketplace with blood from the tripe dripping down his back, the stench of it clogging his senses. Rattled and humiliated, Hassan covered all the routes through town as per his master's instructions. When he returned to the Sufi lodge, Shaykh Abu Sa'id told him: *"Now go back and ask people if they saw you when you passed them carrying the tripe."* Hassan went to the marketplace again but was surprised when no one recalled him passing them earlier. Confused by the whole incident, he returned to Shaykh Abu Sa'id, who said: *"The only person who looked at you was you because your ego was upset. My son, you are of no concern to anyone else."* The Shaykh then asked for the tripe to be cooked that night and said to the devotees: *"O Brothers! Enjoy this tripe, for indeed Hassan's ego will be cooked with it."*

It was not long before Hassan was given a further lesson in subduing his ego. One day, during heavy rainfall, Shaykh Abu Sa'id told his devotees to go and play in the water that had pooled up. All the devotees, except Khwaja Abu Bakr, jumped into the water. He felt this was a frivolous thing, and he did not want to ruin his clothes. While he stood by judging the others, Hassan snuck up behind him, placed his head between his legs, lifted him up and then chucked him in the water. But this instantly became a problem because Khwaja Abu Bakr did not know how to swim. He flailed with great difficulty before the others finally pulled him out. They turned him upside down to let the water drain from his lungs.

Further mockery followed when Shaykh Abu Sa'id and the devotees performed funeral rites over Khwaja Abu Bakr while he was clearly still alive. The Shaykh then spoke: *"O Abu Bakr, arise from the dead and speak."* Afterwards, having been helped onto his donkey, Abu Bakr left for home. That evening, as was the custom, the devotees gathered for their communal dinner - but on this occasion, Shaykh Abu Sa'id did not join them.

The next morning, Shaykh Abu Sa'id summoned Hassan and sent him on a mission. *"You must go to Balkh. It will take you twelve days there and twelve to return, but you must be back here on the twenty-fifth day. Go there and meet Amir Khusrau, give him my greetings, ask him for three tons of fragrance-wood and pay off the debt we owe him."* The journey did not go as smoothly as Hassan expected, as he was captured by Turks who mistook him for a spy. He was severely beaten and robbed of his possessions and clothes. Eventually, he requested spiritual support, and then the commander-in-chief of the Turks appeared. He had Hassan's limbs untied, and his clothes returned. He explained to Hassan that he had just had a dream in which an elegant man holding a sword threatened him with his life unless he untied Hassan. Hassan understood this to be his Shaykh, and so, after a short respite, he resumed his journey. Finally arriving in Balkh, he found that Amir Khusrau was not present and had gone away for an indefinite period . By this point, Hassan was deflated and exhausted. However, he knew that he must return home before the twenty-fifth day. So, immediately, he set off on his return journey.

Upon arriving back, he was greeted by all the devotees and the Shaykh himself, who remarked: *"Hassan, do you want to tell the story or shall I?"* *"It is better heard from the Shaykh"*, Hassan replied. Shaykh Abu Sa'id then regaled the whole story to the other devotees. He then looked at Hassan and said, *"I knew you would not find Amir Khusrau in Balkh. Your ego, which was still big enough to lift Abu Bakr and throw him into the water, needed the stick of a Turk. It was too big for me to discipline, so I sent you for the purpose of subduing your ego."*

Subduing the ego is an important stage in becoming a good servant. One must simply be courteous in all one's actions and responses. Until the ego becomes a servant to the soul's needs, it will remain difficult to truly serve, as the ego will always find a way to interfere. Therefore, Shaykh Abu Sa'id continuously put

Hassan through his paces. He was aware that the young man may have borne the roots of love in his heart. He still needed an occasional nudge to accelerate his inner transformation. In this way, we may say that a person with love for his master must make relatively little effort in physical terms. Still, a tremendous amount of progress will need to occur regarding that person's ego.

On another day, Shaykh Abu Sa'id instructed Hassan to go to the local police chief and tell him to pay for a feast for the darwishes. Hassan set off thinking to himself: *"There is no one in Nishapur who is more opposed to the shaykh than him, but these are my orders, so I must obey."* When he reached the police station, he found the chief busy beating up a detainee whose bag of coins had been confiscated.

Hassan conveyed Abu Sa'id's message, but the chief mocked him and uttered some obscenities. He then threw the bag of coins at him, exclaiming: *"Maybe the shaykh would like to treat the darwishes with this confiscated money."* He returned with the bag of coins and mentioned what had happened to Shaykh Abu Sa'id. He was then told to use the coins to prepare a meal for the darwishes. Some devotees questioned the shaykh's judgement, but Hassan remained steadfastly loyal to his orders. After the food had been prepared and served, Shaykh Abu Sa'id noticed no one was eating. So he said: *"Bismillah, start eating."* Although the table remained unenthused, everyone gradually started eating, knowing their food had been purchased with that dubious bag of coins.

At a gathering the next day, a young person stood up in front of the shaykh and began to plead for forgiveness. He told him: *"I have betrayed you. When my father was about to die, he gave me two bags of coins and instructed me to give one bag as a gift to you, but I decided to keep both. Yesterday, as I walked in the bazaar, the police chief took me away and beat me. Then he took that bag of coins which was rightfully yours, and threw it at someone. I am offering you my share now because I realise the beating was a punishment from God for withholding what was rightfully yours."* Shaykh Abu Sa'id replied: *"Keep what is yours but do not deny the rights of others."* The police chief was later informed about what had transpired. As

Hassan had shocked him with his perfect etiquette and patience whilst dealing with his unsavoury behaviour, the police chief too came to Shaykh Abu Sa'id and sought his forgiveness.

The servant is the ambassador of the shaykh. As such, he must be as true a reflection of the shaykh's personality as possible. If he were to appear coarse in his conversations, he would create a coldness in the people's hearts towards the shaykh. This would mean that he would be depriving his own shaykh of valuable service and be guilty of denying people the chance to obtain blessings through the shaykh.

On another occasion, Shaykh Abu Sa'id kept sending Hassan to the shop of one of his loyal devotees, Abu Umar. At sunset, the Shaykh told Hassan: *"Go again to Abu Umar and ask him to give you some fragrances."* Hassan was embarrassed when he arrived at the shop, as this would be the eighth time he had been on that day. Abu Umar said: *"Why are you afraid to ask? Why do you feel embarrassed? Even if the shaykh were to order me to give a thousand dinars, I would not hesitate."* These words were a source of encouragement for Hassan, lifting the burden from his heart. He vowed to himself that he would never hesitate to carry out the shaykh's duties in the future. When he returned, Shaykh Abu Sa'id said to him: *"Hassan. Clean your inside and your outside so you can sit with the holy ones."* Hassan came out from this meeting crying. He began to rub dust on his face, asking for forgiveness.

Hassan became steadfast and firm in his conviction of his master's wisdom. Whatever task was assigned to him, he tried to fulfil it to the best of his ability - even when logic, reason, or the chance of success were not immediately obvious. He selflessly committed all his resources and energy to perform service for his master and the rest of mankind. He understood that this was a service lacking any immediate payment or acknowledgement. As Shaykh Sa'di (1210–1290) remarks: *"The path is nothing but service to others."*

Moreover, it is an honour on the servant's part that, out of all mankind, he alone has been chosen to fulfil this role. If anyone could offer a servant payment for his service, the servant would and should look upon it as an insult. Similarly, in the famous story of Khidr and Moses, there is a moment in which both heroes go their separate ways. After Khidr has repaired the orphans' decrepit wall, Moses points out that the local people had been consistently unfriendly to them. He could not understand how Khidr could continue doing such an act of kindness - he should at the very least be paid for his service. Khidr had patiently accepted previous interferences, but this was the last straw. How could he accept payment for a service when he was carrying it out solely for God's pleasure?

A Sufi master once remarked on one of his servants that: *"Even if a flood goes over his head, he never complains."* The servant's perpetual state must be one of patience and endurance, as the shaykh will subject him to the most challenging situations and present his stoic virtue as an example with which to teach others. A servant must also show discretion in his dealings with the shaykh and with other people. He must never indulge in speaking candidly about matters that concern the shaykh or any others who have entrusted him with their confidence. To do so would jeopardise his standing as a confidant. The Prophet ﷺ once asked his young servant, Anas, to perform a task. While en route to perform it, he met his mother, who asked him where he was going. He remained silent for a while and then told his mother that the Prophet ﷺ had entrusted him with a task, the details of which he could not divulge even to his mother. His mother was overjoyed by the maturity he had shown and said: *"Well done, son. This is how you should be – you should never disclose what the Prophet ﷺ tells you."*

Many other people also performed dutiful service in the lodge of Shaykh Abu Sa'id. Some were wealthy and others destitute, but all performed some service; preparing food, cleaning the rooms or straightening shoes. One devotee, Bu Salih, had the duty of carrying a toothpick for the shaykh. He also carried a pair of scissors to trim his master's moustache. He asserted wonderfully: *"You need to have the knowledge of seventy scholars to know how to trim a moustache."*

On this point, Allama Iqbal (1877–1938) writes: *"If you seek the longing of the love of God, then serve the faqirs (pious people) because this pearl is not found in the treasures of kings."* This is because the pious people live in constant remembrance of their Lord. Even tasks such as trimming the moustache can become tedious and time-consuming. So here, from the Almighty's endless mercy, He has created vacancies for those not busy in remembrance to serve His people so that they may attain something of their purity.

One day Imam Qushayri (986–1074) was performing a shower when he ran out of water. He called out: *"Is there any student around to pour more water through the water hole?"* Shaykh Abu Ali Farmadi heard Imam Qushayri's voice and sprinted to assist him. Imam Qushayri enquired: *"Which student is it?"* He heard the reply: *"It's Abu Ali."* Imam Qushayri responded: *"O Abu Ali, what I have attained in sixty years of hardship, you have gained in pouring that one bucket of water."*

As a dedicated servant, Hassan was entrusted with greater responsibility than others. On several occasions, he found himself in dire situations. As a servant, one recurrent problem throughout his time was the many debts he would accrue through performing his role, as the following story illustrates. One day, Shaykh Abu Sa'id told his son, Shaykh Abu Tahir, and Hassan to make a sweet dish. Hassan was worried because he had no money. Still, as he and Shaykh Abu Tahir made their way to the market, a person came running towards them and exclaimed: *"I was looking for you! Our caravan was attacked by some bandits earlier, and I made a pledge that if we were saved, I would give one full sack of potatoes to the shaykh."* Other people then came forward to Shaykh Abu Tahir and Hassan with similar tales of their pledges. Some donated money, and others gave semolina flour to make the sweet dish.

On another day, Shaykh Abu Sa'id said to his servant: *"Hassan, rise to your feet."* He stood up, and Shaykh Abu Sa'id said to him: *"I want you to know that I did not call you unto myself; I called you unto your non-existence."* Hassan replied: "Master, is existence enough?" Hassan comprehended that these words from his master carried an important message. All the service he had done towards his master had served a purpose: it had prepared him to be a servant of God.

Hassan understood that Shaykh Abu Sa'id did not have long to live. Therefore, he was instructing him to be a servant of God for the remainder of his life.

Following this, Shaykh Abu Sa'id decided to give his followers a final message. He told Hassan to saddle a horse for him. He then rode around the local area, saying farewell to all the people. He bade farewell to all the trees and caves, visiting all the places he had performed seclusions. Hassan narrates the last episode: *"I was walking in attendance of the shaykh and thinking to myself that 'after the shaykh's death, I will have to be the one to arrange everything. My heart was greatly concerned with the debts of my service - what will happen when the shaykh is gone? The master sensed I was burdened and said to me: 'Hassan, do not trouble your heart over debts, for God will send someone three days after my death and set your heart free from the debts.' Lo and behold, three days after the blessed death of my master, a man arrived and paid off every last debt."*

The legacy of Hassan is reflected in the fact that no books were ever written on him. This is an honour for a servant, as his acclaim lies in being remembered well by the master he served. As it befits his rank of Khadim-e Khas, Hassan is buried near Shaykh Abu Sa'id in the same tomb in Meyhana, Turkmenistan.

"The path is nothing but service to others."

Abu Sa'id ﷺ

الحفيظ

The Preserver

DIVINE PROTECTION

Imam Nawawi (1233–1277)

Imam Nawawi is a renowned Shafi'i hadith scholar, equally admired by the Sufis and non-Sufis. I have taught two of his works, Riyad Al-Salihin and Al-Arba'in, to many students over the decades. I personally love his commitment to Islam and his modest lifestyle. This article was written by Majid and Saqib in 2011.

The Prophet ﷺ said: *"There are seven whom God will shade with His shade on the Day when there is no shade but His shade: a just ruler; a youth who grows up worshipping God, the Mighty and Exalted; a man whose heart is attached to the mosque; two men who love each other for the sake of God, meeting and parting for that reason alone; a man who refuses the advances of a noble and beautiful woman, saying, 'I fear God'; a man who gives in charity and conceals it so that his left-hand does not know what his right-hand gives; and a man who remembers God when he is alone so that his eyes overflow with tears."*

As such, there are seven kinds of people who will attain God's protection on the Day of Judgement. On that day, every soul will be seeking safety from the intensity of the sun's heat, and a person's own sweat will be enough to drown him. On that day, God's promise of shade and protection will be the ultimate prize.

Though it may seem to be an unachievable feat at first glance, if we look closer, the categories of conduct for whom this protection will be inevitable are not beyond the realm of any ordinary individual. We might be excused for thinking that these categories are the realms solely for the holy people. But this is not the case, as their achievement is well within an individual's capacity. For instance, to give charity, whilst concealing it from others, is obviously a daily task and aspiration. And it is plausible that such a charitable person may also be wholeheartedly attached to the mosque. God's greatest and most pious, holy servants can so easily fit into all of these categories. They can do so because they implicitly understand that they must always strive to shape their behaviour following these ideals to achieve God's protection on that day. In the Hereafter, they are utterly obliged to seek that protection. This elusive protection always surrounds us in the material world. Yet, we remain totally unaware of it, forcing us to increase our desire to seek it. To attain higher levels of this protection, we must first enhance our awareness about its various forms and guises. Then, we must appreciate its existence, or non-existence, in our lives.

This is exemplified in Imam Yahya Ibn Sharaf's life, Imam Nawawi, born in Nawa (present-day Horan, Syria) in 1233. He came from a pious family; his father Sharaf was a poor merchant and a hidden saint. When Yahya was seven years old, he woke up on the night of the 27th of Ramadan. He realised that the room was filled with light. He awoke his father and asked him: *"Father, what is this light filling up the room?"* His parents awoke and did not see any light. They realised that their son had witnessed the Night of Power.

One day, Sharaf was visited by Shaykh Yasin Ibn Yusuf, who advised him: *"Look after your son, for he will have a promising future. One day he will become an incredibly knowledgeable and pious person. The people will benefit from him."* Sharaf was not acquainted with Shaykh Yasin and was surprised by this instruction. He enquired if Shaykh Yasin was a fortune teller. Shaykh Yasin replied negatively and then related to him the following incident: *"I was passing nearby Nawa when I witnessed something rare. I saw this ten-year-old boy (Yahya) sitting on a bridge reading a book. His friends kept asking him to play with them, but he refused and continued to read his book. Then his friends tried to pull him down, but the boy refused. He began to cry to get them to leave him alone. I was amazed at the dedication of the boy and so decided to approach him. When I came close, I observed that he was reciting the Holy Qur'an. I then had an inspired notion from God that this boy would become a great person. I enquired about his family and was told that he was your son. I wanted to tell you, so you can be aware and look after him closely."* Sharaf took Shaykh Yasin's advice to heart and gave special attention to his son's upbringing. Yahya memorised the Qur'an, then, at the age of eighteen, he asked his father's permission to move to Damascus - the hub of the world's knowledge. As the Prophet ﷺ mentioned: *"Angels spread their wings for the seeker of knowledge."*

Imam Nawawi said: *"To seek knowledge is one of the best preoccupations, and one of the best pursuits to bring you near to God, and one of the best teachers of obedience."* In 1251, Yahya moved from Nawa to Damascus and enrolled to study at the Madrasa Saramiyya. However, there was presently no accommodation for him. His teacher advised him to join the madrasa Rahwahiyyah instead, named after the great hadith master Imam Ishaq Ibn Rahwayh (777–852). Here, he occupied a small room for many years. Despite its size, he filled it to bursting with books. The only way a guest could sit down in it was to pile the books on top of each other to make room for himself. Imam Nawawi commented: *"I studied in this institution for two years. During my stay, I never had complete rest and lived on the limited food supplied by the institution."*

During this period, Imam Nawawi accompanied his father to perform Hajj. Along the way, he visited Madinah and other sacred places. He returned to Damascus, where he continued his studies and memorised the crucial texts of the Shafi'i school. He studied under many acclaimed scholars in the mosques of Damascus. He had twelve lessons daily, and it was his practice to memorise his books by heart while walking along the street on his way to and from lessons.

Along with this intensive practice, he still miraculously found time to compile notes and explanations of every lesson and show them to his teachers the following day. His intelligence, hard work, love and devotion to his studies amazed his teachers. They became fond of him. The hadith expert Imam Al-Dhahabi (1274–1348) notes: *"His (Imam Nawawi's) dedication to learning, night and day, became proverbial."*

Imam Nawawi showed such devotion to knowledge that he ensured his closeness to God. Later recorded that: *"Imam Nawawi only slept when sleep overcame him - he slept reading his books. On waking up, he would lament the time he had wasted sleeping."* Imam Nawawi exerted all his effort in gaining sacred knowledge. This practice continued for six years. In that period, he became proficient in the science of the Prophet's ﷺ traditions and became well-versed in jurisprudence and Arabic. Imam Nawawi remarked that: *"Scholars agree that to be preoccupied in seeking knowledge is better than voluntary acts. Voluntary acts only benefit the person who does them, whereas knowledge can reach and benefit other people."*

At the age of twenty-four, he was uniquely blessed with the ability to spread knowledge and guide others. And so, Imam Nawawi became one of the 'true heirs of the prophets'. This was a blessed title bestowed on the people of knowledge, as they were seen as the cause of the masses being led to the right path. The people themselves loved Imam Nawawi and frequently attended his religious sessions to learn and listen to his eloquent speech.

He would spend the next twenty years of his life writing and teaching the knowledge of Islam in the mosques. He held different prominent religious positions, the highest one being in the Ashrafiyya School of Damascus' prophetic traditions. The scholars before Imam Nawawi had compiled forty distinct traditions of thought: *"Whoever preserves for my ummah forty hadith related to the religion, God will resurrect him in the company of the scholars."* Nawawi's collection of the *'Forty Prophetic Traditions'* is still considered the most popular work of scholarship from the era and is still widely read worldwide. In this work, he begins his observations with a beautiful introduction promoting the importance of following the Sunnah, stating: *"What the Messenger gives, [you must] take, and what he forbids abstain from it."*

The first tradition compiled by Imam Nawawi in his collection reads like this:

'*Actions are but by intentions, and every man shall have only what he intended.*'
He begins this way to place a special emphasis on the importance of sincere
intentions. A person may not possess much factual knowledge, but because of
good intentions, he will gain protection. In his famous work, *Riyad Al-Salihin
(Garden of the Pious)*, Imam Nawawi acted upon the following tradition. This
work's immense popularity is such that it can also be found in mosques
worldwide and translated into dozens of languages. Anas Ibn Malik narrates
that the Prophet ﷺ said: "*None of you [truly] believes until he wishes for his
brother what he wishes for himself.*" Nawawi was the epitome of a well-wisher
of Muslims. It was his intention to ensure that other Muslims benefited from
God's protection.

Suppose we follow the teachings of Imam Nawawi and declare a wholehearted
intention to follow the Sunnah ourselves. In that case, we will ensure that we
receive protection from God. Increasing the sincerity of our intentions would
allow us to benefit from the other traditions Imam Nawawi compiles in his
'*Forty Prophetic Traditions.*' These traditions clearly and concisely guide us on
the importance and virtue of following the five pillars of Islam: the need to purify
the heart (concerned with beneficial matters and avoiding doubtful acts); the
need for good manners and the obligation for loving Muslims; doing charitable
and good deeds; the concept of taqwa (fear of God); and the need for seeking
God's forgiveness through repentance.

The following tradition compiled by Imam Nawawi summarises the fundamental
insight that we must remember God to gain protection. Abdullah Ibn Abbas
says: "*One day I was sitting behind the Prophet ﷺ, and he said to me: "Young
man, I shall teach you some words [of advice]: Be mindful of God, He will protect
you. Be mindful of God, and you will find Him in front of you. If you ask, ask of God;
if you seek help, seek the help of God. Know that if the nation were to gather, to
benefit you with anything, it would gift you only with something God had already
prescribed for you. Suppose they gather to harm you with anything. In that case,
they will harm you only with something God had already prescribed for you. The
pens have been lifted, and the pages have dried.*"

Muslims have a certain level of protection surrounding them solely due to their belief in Islam. They have accepted God and His Messenger ﷺ. This protection that surrounds all Muslims is a lifelong safety net for us. Still, it is immediately lifted when we fail to appreciate this shield of protection and abuse it. The biggest danger in this case, which can be termed a kind of 'spiritual suicide', is thus created when we show a lack of appreciation for this protection. We end up purposefully performing destructive acts, as we have attached no significance to the protection we've always been afforded. In that scenario, we then lose our safeguard when any other situation arises.

Conversely, we remain unaware that we encounter so many opportunities to strengthen this shield of protection in our day-to-day lives. For example, when we make ablution, we ensure that we maintain cleanliness and purity. However, in the state of ablution, we are also protected from the whisperings of the devil. We also attain protection when we perform acts of worship to fulfil the obligations of Islam. Performing prayer, keeping fasts and giving to charity are all intended to act towards our personal protection. Additionally, all these acts are done in remembrance of God.

The *awliya* themselves constantly seek the protection of God as they possess something precious – true faith. In the last section of his book, *Bustan Al-Arifin*, *(Garden of the Knowers of God)*, Imam Nawawi explains that the *awliya* are not sinless like the prophets; they are, instead, protected. He explains that this is the greatest miracle for a saint. To be chosen by God is to be protected from sin. Having the ability to do such good deeds until death is the cause and effect of God's protection. And since the awliya are protected, they are the ones to guide people's hearts towards God.

However, in this regard, it is foolish to assume that satan will stay asleep and leave our iman safe. On the contrary, as it is the most precious thing we possess, he will attempt to take it away from us, especially on the brink of death. A master from Bhopal in India mentions: *"Every area I visited, I would go and find a master and then ask for his protection. I would say: 'Master, I am blind, please be* my guide. I am deaf; be my ears. I am lame; be my legs. I am incapacitated; please be my hands.'"

Imam Al-Dhahabi records: "*Imam Nawawi devoted his life to religious knowledge. He was a very pious scholar who had renounced worldly pleasures and was content with an ascetic life.*" His student and close companion, Ibn Al-Attar, said: "*Imam Nawawi had a black beard with a few grey hairs and was often mistaken for a farmer for his torn clothes. His wardrobe consisted just of a turban and an ankle-length shirt. [He] was a devout worshipper and regularly fasted. He had one meal and drank water once in the day.*"

Imam Nawawi was once offered a peeled cucumber to eat, but he refused it, as he was worried that if he were to eat it, he would relax and feel tired. Damascus was famed at the time for its delicious and diverse types of fruit. However, Imam Nawawi renounced all fruit, as most of Damascus' orchards had been donated to children whose parents had died or left them empty and bereaved. The guardians of those orphans were trading in the fruits of these orchards, doubtfully. Imam Nawawi was thus adhering to this following tradition of the Prophet ﷺ: "*O God, I consider it a sin not to protect the rights of the two weak ones; orphans and women.*"

It was Imam Nawawi's practice throughout his adult life to spend the night in prayer. Once, a man entered the Umayyad mosque and found Imam Nawawi praying behind a pillar. The man listened to him weeping in deep submission to God and repeating one Qur'anic verse: "*And halt them to be questioned,*" for a long time. The man was deeply moved.

Imam Nawawi enjoined the good and forbade the evil. When Sultan Baybars became the absolute ruler, he seized some orchards in Damascus, claiming to support his army. Imam Nawawi sent the sultan a private message, expressing his respect for him as a ruler and explaining the conduct that befitted him in the present situation. Sultan Baybars was a brave horseman, full of pride and arrogance, so he did not accept Imam Nawawi's message and angrily reprimanded him.

However, Imam Nawawi did not worry about his own well-being; he only cared about pleasing God. He reprimanded Sultan Baybars right back and informed him that it was the eternal duty of Muslim scholars to defend Islam. Therefore, he could not remain silent in the face of injustice. He advised the sultan that his own responsibility was towards the welfare of the people. In reply, Sultan Baybars reprimanded Imam Nawawi again. He then peppered his rage with mentions of the great deeds he had done. In response, Imam Nawawi reminded Sultan Baybars that he had done nothing beyond his plain duty as his people's ruler. He advised him to remember God.

Imam Nawawi was a pious and ascetic worshipper, and he always abstained from worldly pleasures and desires. He had always been eager to acquire the knowledge of Islam and had dedicated himself wholeheartedly to the worship of God. He had urged the right, forbade the wrong and made great contributions to the world he was born into. The fact that he accomplished all of this before he reached forty-five is truly remarkable. When his death was approaching, God gave him a clear sign. So he journeyed to Damascus to say his farewells to his close friends and remind them to fear God. He returned the books he had borrowed from charitable donations, visited the graves of his masters, and then finally departed - going first to Jerusalem then to his native Nawa. Within a week of his homecoming, he became ill at his father's house. He died in the year 1277. However, Imam Nawawi has lived on in Muslims' hearts ever since, as his many works remain treasure troves of knowledge from which millions of readers and scholars have benefited.

A person from our mosque happened to visit Imam Nawawi's shrine. He relates his experience:

"It was a two-hour journey from Damascus for our group to reach Nawa. The graveyard was situated in the centre of the town. It was just a short distance away from the main mosque, which was named after Imam Nawawi. The shrine of Imam Nawawi was in the centre of the graveyard and was fortified by high tiled walls. Upon entering the shrine, we all noticed this beautiful tree, whose branches reached

above the walls. When we enquired about the grave, the servant pointed to the root of the tree. We were all surprised to learn that this was the grave of Imam Nawawi. We had visited other shrines during our stay in Syria and had not seen anything like this. A huge tree emerged from within the grave, just a plot of land and had no headstone. The tree's bark was not visible, but the tree's roots spread and grew many branches above the soil's surface. The servant mentioned that the tree was seven hundred years old. It was an amazing sight, and although I had seen photos of the shrine beforehand, I realised that no photo could capture the atmosphere of this shrine. In my mind, I imagined the trunk of the tree reaching into the grave and visualised Imam Nawawi leaning against it. While we sat there and read our litanies, I was also busy in thought, trying to figure out the tree's symbolic meaning. Meanwhile, one of my companions had been busy with similar thoughts and counted the tree's branches. He counted twenty large branches and concluded that each branch represented each year Imam Nawawi taught for, as he had taught for twenty years. We sat for a couple of hours and felt at peace. Although there was no shelter, we did our best to avoid the rain. The servant was a pleasant gentleman who gave us gifts and some cuttings of plants that had been growing on the tree."

The story of the life of Imam Nawawi teaches us that, as he was mindful of God during his youth, God protected him during his adult years. Imam Nawawi's relationship with God was special from his earliest days. This devotion remained a constant throughout his life. Imam Nawawi was ultimately given the title 'Muhyiddin', which means someone who revives the religion. When this was mentioned to him, he said: *"God forbid! Who am I to revive the religion? Religion does not need me or anybody else!"*

"To seek knowledge is one of the best preoccupations and one of the best things which takes you near to God and one of the best for obedience."

Imam Nawawi

The Extender

LOYALTY

Miran Bhikh (1629–1714)

It was Miran Bhikh's vernacular poetry that initially attracted me to him. I later studied his life and realised that he was a sincere devotee of his master. He remains a role model, particularly for the devotee who wishes to remain loyal to his master. This article was written in 2012 by Sayyid Amjid, Rauf and Afdal.

Our virtues constitute our lives' purpose, the contents of our character and the truest expressions of our spiritual state. Mercy, love and compassion are our go-to examples of virtues. However, there is one outstanding virtue, loyalty. Loyalty is the foundation from which all other admirable characteristics stem. If you do not plant the root, then how will you pick the fruit? Loyalty is the habit of devoting your life to a higher purpose. For the one striving along the path to God, everything revolves around loyalty. True loyalty is that devotion that is inherent to your nature. Having true loyalty, you would not know how to be disloyal, even if you tried. Abu Bakr did not know how to be disloyal to the Prophet ﷺ. During his caliphate Abu Bakr (573–634) safeguarded the Sunnah of the Prophet ﷺ. Spiritual matters can only be transmitted from heart to heart. Mawlana Rumi (1207–1273) remarks: *"Some birds cannot digest gems, and you are doing injustice to them by offering them pearls."* The people who maintain a firm connection with their shaykh are always blessed with divine grace and remain vigilant. They keep an eye on their ego. These people build their lives on the virtue of loyalty and show off the characteristics of love and sincerity. Such people remember the goodness done to them, and so they live as great examples of loyalty.

One great-grandson of the Prophet ﷺ in this regard was Miran Bhikh, a descendant of Imam Husayn. His greatest ancestor, Sayyid Ahmad, resided in Tirmidh, Uzbekistan. Miran Bhikh was born to Sayyid Muhammad Yusuf in 1629. He was first named Sayyid Muhammad Sa`id and later became known as Miran Bhikh. He was very fond of his father, who granted him much love and affection and paid great attention to his development. However, his father died when he was ten years old, causing him a wave of pain and anguish that he could not bear to undergo at home – so he ran away into the jungle. His brother, Jan Muhammad, set out on a recovery mission and eventually found him living in the wilderness. After he regained some strength at home, his mother asked him to continue his studies and honour his father's wishes.

Nevertheless, Miran Bhikh still could not bear to stay at home. His father's absence from his life was too painful. He mentioned this to his mother and asked her permission to study abroad. His mother gave him permission and then packed him off to meet his first teacher, Akhund Farid. On one occasion, Shaykh Jamal, a great saint, passed through the area and noticed Miran Bhikh playing with other children. He called all the children one by one and asked his companions about each child. When he came to Miran Bhikh, the people told him that he was Sayyid Muhammad Yusuf's son. Shaykh Jamal called his teacher, Akhund Farid, and gave him five rupees, saying: *"Take great care and look after this child. Indeed, one day he will become the spiritual pole."*

Even at such an early age, Miran Bhikh was intelligent and devoted to his studies and surpassed many older students. One day a soothsayer visited the madrasa. Upon seeing Miran Bhikh, he immediately foretold: *"One day this child will grow up to become such a great man that he will appear like a king to his people. He will be surrounded by thousands, all seeking his blessings."*

After completing his education with Akhund Farid, Miran Bhikh spent almost one whole year in the presence of a saint - Miyan Muhammad Qasim. His duties included preparing warm water for other students and for the people who came to pray in the mosque. To keep the stove heated, he had to collect wood from the jungle. Some students and devotees of Muhammad Qasim went to the jungle to find a large tree trunk to use as a beam on the house built for the shaykh. After the beam was prepared and cut to size, it so happened that it was still too heavy to be lifted. All the students together could not manage to lift the beam, and so Miran Bhikh said: *"Let me try."* He read *"Bismillah hir Rahman nir Rahim,"* then lifted the beam and carried it to the house by himself. However, when the beam was placed on the pillars, it was short and did not reach both walls. Again, Miran Bhikh asked if he could solve the issue, and he lifted the beam and put it in place. As he touched the beam, it expanded, and this time stretched to fit perfectly across the ceiling, resting on the walls. Witnessing such miraculous events, Muhammad Qasim told him: *"You are meant for something else, and your share is with someone else."* Miran Bhikh asked him: *"O Master, please guide me because I do not know who to look for and where to go."* Muhammad Qasim then instructed him that he would find his destiny fulfilled at Shaykh Abu Mali's hand. With Muhammad Qasim's permission, Miran Bhikh went to Shaykh Abu Mali, who then initiated him into the Qadiriyya and Chishtiyya order. The Shaykh explained the etiquette of the orders and how to make dhikr before giving him permission to leave.

On one occasion, Miran Bhikh went into the presence of his shaykh's wife, Bibi Sahiba. He asked about the matter that was obviously worrying her. As her daughter was ready to be married off, she told him that many lingering issues needed to be sorted out. Her main concern was the house itself, which was unavoidably dilapidated. So Miran Bhikh gathered two other devotees and immediately got to work, making repairs to the house. After reconstructing the walls, he would bring wood from the jungle as new beams and fix the roof. He continued to fast during the day and only ate boiled lentils without salt in the evenings. As well as attending to these practical matters, he still maintained his daily litanies and his prayers and paid his respects to his shaykh whenever he got the opportunity. Although he was weak due to these rigorous disciplines, his devotion to his shaykh's family had never been greater. After all the work had finally been completed, Bibi Sahiba called her husband and showed him what Miran Bhikh had done. Shaykh Abu Mali was incredibly pleased and prayed: "O God, for the sake of the Prophet ﷺ, grant us success."

Within the context of a relationship, loyalty is when you maintain love and respect for a person. You honour the relationship with your good intentions, true love, and sheer sincerity. You do whatever it takes to maintain these devotions without hesitation or doubt. You aspire to become like the example of Abu Bakr – a man of his word. Loyalty to your master should be automatic. If you have a master, you must be loyal, or nothing happens. However, the more difficult aspect of this is being loyal to your master's children and family. Once, Shaykh Abu Mali's family had to go without food for seven days. Eventually, a few devotees arrived from Saharanpur, near Delhi. Upon noticing the situation, they decided that something had to be done. They knew Shaykh Abu Mali would be offended if they offered any direct financial help. So it was decided instead to invite him and his devotees to Saharanpur. This way, they could serve him out of their hospitality. Shaykh Abu Mali accepted the invitation, and so he travelled to Saharanpur with his entourage. Every day a different household hosted the group, and each did their utmost to prepare a good feast for their guests. Since it was Miran Bhikh's duty to serve and distribute the food at every meal, he would first make sure that some food was put away to one side before serving the guests. Once the food had been distributed and everyone had finished eating, he took the food he'd put aside and walked eighteen miles to his master's house. Upon arriving late at night, he awoke the rest of the shaykh's family and then presented them with the food. After that, he would gather the empty pots and return to Saharanpur to arrive before Tahajjud to bring Shaykh Abu Mali water to make ablution. Miran Bhikh did this three times daily. This visit continued for twenty days, and he maintained taking food for the family for the entirety of its duration.

Upon returning home, Shaykh Abu Mali reunited with his family. He asked them how they had miraculously managed in his absence since he had left them with no money or food. They replied that they had been well looked after. *"We ate what you ate."*, they told him. Shaykh Abu Mali asked what they meant by this and was told: *"Every day, Miran Bhikh brought us some food back from wherever you were staying. Thus, we were also partaking in the same food that you were served."* This truly touched his heart, and so he prayed: *"O God, make him one of Your accepted servants. Grant him the light and Your understanding so we can be happy with this son of a sayyid and fulfil our obligation."*

On another occasion, one of the walls in the house needed repairing. Shaykh Abu Mali ordered Miran Bhikh to take responsibility for the matter. He also asked another devotee to watch over Miran Bhikh and report back on his progress. Miran Bhikh called a builder and explained what needed to be done; meanwhile, the devotee shadowed him closely. Once, he followed him as he walked into the jungle, and he watched while a very handsome young man riding a horse approached Miran Bhikh. As the devotee looked towards the horseman's face, he was blinded by a strong light and suddenly fainted. When he eventually regained consciousness, he rushed to see Shaykh Abu Mali. He reported all that had happened, saying: *"All I remember is seeing the rider give five rupees to Miran Bhikh. After fainting, I was unable to see or hear what happened between that rider and Miran Bhikh. I am sorry, master - that person was so handsome that I fainted, and when I came around, he had gone."*

What had happened was that Miran Bhikh had asked for help from the hidden saints. Thus, one of them had come to give him money, which he in turn used to pay the builder. Shaykh Abu Mali called Miran Bhikh and told him: *"Look, son, it is not good to take money from the unseen. Fix the wall yourself, and do not involve anyone else. You already know that the prophets may openly display miracles, but the awliya must keep them hidden."* Sticking to this advice, Miran Bhikh started doing all the work on the house on his own, and this action soon brought many blessings to the house. This was the lesson that Shaykh Abu Mali was trying to teach him. A builder would do the work solely to get paid for it. However, if Miran Bhikh did it himself, he would carry out the exact same task with far more devotion and respect. This authenticity would then inevitably bring blessings to the building and the people who lived in it.

An ounce of loyalty is worth many pounds of cleverness. How does one attain the master's blessing? By doing things to attain his pleasure. After this episode, Shaykh Abu Mali gave Miran Bhikh his cloak, turban, cap and shawl. Miran Bhikh told him: *"O Master, I am not worthy of carrying this burden."* Shaykh Abu Mali replied: *"I am giving it to you, and you are making excuses. Take what is being given. Wearing this robe carries with it the responsibility to live and behave like a darwish; to live a simple and humble life; to endure poverty, hunger, and struggles; and apply great effort and hard work. For a darwish, happiness and sadness are the same. The darwish must love the poor, destitute and needy."*

Miyan Muhammad Ishaq tells his own revealing story: *"Once it came to my heart that since Miran Bhikh had become a big shaykh, he had not appointed anyone to succeed him. Was it that there was no one capable? Or did he not want to give it to anyone and keep it solely for himself? These thoughts troubled me. Then I had a dream in which I saw a large gathering. I saw that many people were coming and entering this gathering. I also wanted to enter, but I was refused, and so I stood to one side. After a while, I approached a darwish, and, after much begging and pleading, he started to take me with him. We were halted by the gatekeepers and were told that I could not enter because I bore doubts and did not hold a firm belief. However, the Darwish interceded for me, and we entered the gathering. Once inside, I saw the Prophet ﷺ seated at the head of the gathering. I asked the darwish about this gathering's purpose. I was told that prophet Yusuf wanted to meet Miran Bhikh and had expressed this to the Prophet ﷺ. At that moment, Miran Bhikh came and expressed great humility to the Prophet ﷺ. The Prophet ﷺ treated him with a lot of kindness and then told him that the prophet Yusuf desired to meet him. Then from one corner, prophet Yusuf appeared. Miran Bhikh stood up out of respect, embraced him and met him with great respect and honour. Prophet Yusuf gave him a gift of a turban and some other things. Then the Prophet ﷺ also blessed him with a turban. After a while, he was given permission to leave."*

Miran Bhikh himself says in one poem: *'Bhikh bukkah koi nahi.'* No one is empty; none is without that pearl. The problem is they do not know how to unlock it. If people knew the value of that gift, they would never raise their heads from prostration throughout their life. Everyone is capable of such feats.

'If a person comes to seek God, the shaykhs accept that person, whatever state he may be in, for being a devotee is better than not being a devotee.' *'The shaykh takes the milk and then brings out the curd'* - for purifying the heart, a person needs a shaykh. They simply cannot do it on their own. The shaykh does not ask for money or for rent. All he asserts is that you have now come to him, showing your inspired commitment. The master unlocks your capabilities so that you are learning your own potential all the time. Thus, a loyal person discards all forms of bitterness. He is grateful for all the good that has been bestowed by his shaykh. Even if he serves his shaykh day and night for the rest of his life, he cannot pay for the blessed goodness he has received from him.

There are still occasions, though, when it may be hard to understand why a shaykh is giving extra attention to people who may not appear to deserve it. However, we must remember that shaykhs see what we cannot see. They may just be showing loyalty due to their ancestry or even their pious deserving parents. Naturally, there are many other examples of loyal and disloyal students and devotees throughout Islamic history. People may serve a well-renowned shaykh but still become disloyal to him. In contrast, other people may progress further due to loyalty and gratefulness to a less-renowned shaykh.

A shaykh must essentially be the spiritual centre for his devotee. The devotee has two dangerous enemies: firstly, his own ego and then the devil. We have some idea of how dangerous the ego is but absolutely no idea how dangerous the devil is or could be. Abundant dhikr is one essential protection against these enemies. The second is a strong connection with the shaykh. That serves as a shield for the devotee that the ego and the devil can never breakthrough. Hence a devotee must keep a link with the shaykh and always remain in contact.

One day, before his shaykh arrived at the devotee's house, his son died, and the devotee quickly hid the body, as he simply did not want to make a scene. He had invited the shaykh to his house to join him for a meal, and as they ate, the shaykh casually asked him about his son. The devotee tried changing the subject, but the shaykh asked again. In the end, he conceded to mentioning that his son had died. The shaykh told him: *"Maybe he is sleeping, go and check."* When the father went to see the body of his son, the boy sat up. Today, the trend is exactly the opposite. The general tendency is to heedlessly offload every problem and concern to the shaykh.

It is said that being loyal to a shaykh means that if your shaykh asks for your life, give it without hesitation, and if he asks for your head, you should offer it without any remorse. On the 9th of Muharram, for example, Imam Husayn (626–680) realised his situation's gravity and that there was indeed no solution. A massacre was inevitable. He decided to bring together his beloved devotees and the Ahl Al–Bayt for a final gathering. Imam Husayn said to them: *"I know your loyalty. You have come this far and supported me, but at this stage, I will not hold it against you if you return to your tribes because I cannot find any solution to this problem. I foresee only bloodshed now. So, in the dark of the night, whoever wants to leave has my permission and my blessing to go. It will not be held against you."*

When morning arrived, Imam Husayn looked to see who had left and found that each and every one of his companions were still with him. His devotees were not naive; they also knew what was coming, but still, they would not desert him.

A similar situation famously occurred at Badr, when the Prophet ﷺ asked the Companions, especially the Ansar, who had never been in a battle with the Quraysh, how they saw the group's chances. The Prophet ﷺ and the migrants fought from necessity, as they had just been driven from their homes. The Ansar had no such reason. From the Ansar, Miqdad stood up and said: *"We are not like Moses' followers, that, when difficulties arose, said to their prophet: 'O Moses, you and your Lord can go and fight.' We are not saying that. We say, 'O Prophet ﷺ , you lead, and we shall follow, even if you lead us into the sea, we will follow.'"*

There is a verse in the Qur'an that says: *'Among the believers are men who have proven true to what they pledged to God. Some of them have fulfilled their pledge with their lives...'* (33:23) This is what the Companions did. They fulfilled their promise to the Prophet ﷺ that they would support Islam to their dying breath. God continues: *'Others are waiting their turn...'* (33:23) This, in its turn, is an opening to all Muslims until the end of time.

The Prophet ﷺ had several donkeys, including one called Ya'fur and another called Duldul. He used to tell his donkeys to call on his Companions, and the donkeys would knock their heads on the Companions' door. In this way, the Companions would know that the Prophet ﷺ wished to meet them. When the Prophet ﷺ passed away, the donkeys could not survive their separation from him, and both of them jumped into a well. Each donkey ended its life because it could not live without the Prophet ﷺ. This example shows how loyalty lies not just with human beings but also potentially exists within every creature. There are examples of people leaving their entire estate to their cats or dogs because they see their grandchildren as greedy and insufficiently loyal. They reward the animal instead for its steadfast love. Often too, a horse can be seen to cry because its master has died.

Imam Ja'far Al-Sadiq (702–765) says: *"Do not trust a disloyal person."* A person can be clever, but if he is disloyal, then it is of no benefit. Miran Bhikh says in one of his poems: *"Don't be disloyal, because when a disloyal dog goes from house to house, the response is usually dur (get lost)!"* When you are disloyal to your shaykh or his family, they will tell you to get lost. This is because disloyal people have no allegiance or honour. They have ultimately swapped loyalty for money and other selfish causes. The lowest person is one who has been disloyal to his shaykh. Even though his master has saved, guided and will eventually take care of him in the Hereafter. Like lying or greediness, many other faults may be pardoned, but disloyalty can never be. A loyal person will continue to progress with every intense action and good intention. However, a disloyal person will not progress. Instead, he will simply continue to fall lower.

Hadrat Sahib (1921–2008) said: *"What matters at the end of the day is loyalty."* This is a quality that is present in every figure within this chapter. If you are loyal, you will never be unfortunate. People know in their bones that loyalty is rewarded. If you are loyal to the king, person, or God, you will be rewarded. The people who have a sense know that loyalty is always ultimately beneficial. Miran Bhikh's life was dedicated to his shaykh and his family. It may be difficult to stay loyal to a shaykh's family as they are human beings, flawed as any others. Still, with loyalty, you can stay focused on the greater cause of virtue.

When Miran Bhikh reached eighty-four, he recognised his death was near, although he had no physical illness. Miran Bhikh went out to meet his followers for a farewell meeting. He gave his deputies loving advice to look after his people, feed them well, and keep their traditions alive. He finally advised: *"When people come to you, treat them with respect. Do not neglect to win their hearts. Deal with them as a compulsory obligation and not as a trivial duty. This is a major responsibility."* Some holy people have remarked that only the awliya and those linked with them will remain safe when trials and tribulations occur. In difficult times those people nearest the centre of His shadow will be protected.

"*Do not be disloyal.
When a disloyal dog
goes from house to house,
the response is usually
'dur' (get lost).*"

Miran Bhikh

The Unique

DUNYA - OTHER THAN GOD

Sultan Bahu (1630–1691)

The poetry of Sultan Bahu is still immensely popular in Pakistan and Kashmir. I have always cherished his verses for their great wisdom and sincerity. The handful of lines in particular in which he expresses his love for his master, remain a constant inspiration. This article was written in 2011 by Majid and Saheed.

> *Those who prefer the life of this world to the Hereafter, and bar [others] from the way of God, and seek to make it crooked. They are in extreme error.* (14:3)

The medium of poetry enjoys a high place amongst literary and artistic forms throughout the whole Islamic world. Classics such as the Qasidah Burdah, Sayf ul Muluk or the Mathnawi are memorised at large by people of all classes. The alluring nature of poetry and its rhythmic patterns allowing for ease of memorisation. Subsequently, Sufi saints have successfully employed this medium to convey their message. So intrinsic has poetry become in society that it constitutes a form of transmission. Generation after generation, Islamic beliefs and principles of worship are passed down through poetry.

Nowhere is it more evident than the area now divided between Pakistan and India, called Punjab. The Punjabi life was a simple life where people's time was preoccupied with farming and agriculture. The daily chore of people's lives has served as motifs for the Punjabi poets. The land and its rivers become the context in which the dramatic moments are played. Chores such as washing clothes, fetching water, and grazing animals have become a backdrop in which the Sufi poets have woven their message of the 'Truth'.

Punjab has brought forth many poets - Baba Farid, Shah Husayn, Sultan Bahu and Bulleh Shah, just to name a few. Each one used their voice to emphasise their own imprint of Sufism. Sultan Bahu famously declaimed that the major impediment for all people in attaining spirituality was their attachment to the physical world (dunya). In his view, one must become dead to dunya. Before dying, this quest for death is epitomised in a prophetic saying: *"Die before you die!"*

> *Where one gram of love is sold,*
> *there one should give tons of faith.*
>
> *Books, prayers, and liturgies*
> *should be heaped on top.*
>
> *Nothing is gained without a guide,*
> *even if one stays up nights in the study.*
>
> *Let us die before dying;*
> *Bahu only then is the Lord attained.*

Sultan Bahu developed these central concepts in a manner that proved both appealing and accessible to a wide audience, many of whom were previously unfamiliar with Sufism's more esoteric and philosophical dimensions. His Persian verses have never gained favour in any way comparable to his Punjabi poetry. His fame is almost entirely due to his volumes of the latter, called the Abyat. This work collects his verses arranged in alphabetical order going by the first letter of the Arabo-Persian alphabet. It has always been regarded as one of the greatest treasures of Punjabi literature. In particular, his Punjabi Sufi couplets emphasise the sincerity of all forms of religious devotion, irrespective of religious affiliation. It is no wonder that he is still widely revered by Sikh and Hindu Punjabis just as much as Muslims.

However, information concerning the life of Sultan Bahu is scarce in comparison to many other Sufi figures. Sultan Bahu was born in 1630, during the final years of the Mughal ruler Shah Jahan's reign (he of the Taj Mahal fame) in Shorkot - located between Multan and Jhang in modern-day Pakistan. His family claims a line of descent from Ali, albeit not through Fatimah. His father, Sultan Bayazid Muhammad, was a pious and learned person who had memorised the Qur'an. In recognition of his exemplary military service, he was given the task of managing a crucial fort. He was married to a saintly woman, Bibi Rasti, whose name accurately reflected her state (as rasti means 'to be rightly guided'). Sultan Bayazid was not oblivious to his wife's piety. He considered it his good fortune that although he was still partially attracted by dunya's charm, his saintly wife remained utterly detached.

Bibi Rasti gave her son his overtly mystical name, which literally means 'With Him' or 'The one who is with God'. Bahu kept it as a pen-name, to which his disciples later added Sultan. His full name is Sultan Mahmud Bahu, but he is more commonly referred to as Sultan Bahu. His mother had chosen it in the hope that he would become one of God's special servants:

> *My mother named me Bahu,*
> *hoping I would turn out to be the one who is with God.*

> *Turn Bahu backwards;*
> *the word is Wahab (Grants a lot)*

> *May God's endless Mercy and Compassion be upon my mother 'Rasti,'*
> *Rasti was the one who is rightly guided,*
> *the one who is on the right path.*

Bibi Rasti was a pivotal figure throughout Sultan Bahu's life, especially when his father died when he was a child. Thankfully, the family remained financially secure due to the large inheritance left by his father. It was already evident that this child was extraordinary, and his mother immediately recognised the fact. After his father's death, his mother closely supervised his formal education and spiritual training. Bibi Rasti was aware that many dangers awaited her son in the attraction to dunya. Many people, of course, live and lose their entire lives in pursuit of this world's pleasures. Therefore, she earnestly took it upon herself to wean her son off the physical world and direct him towards the spiritual world. During the formative years, Sultan Bahu observed his mother passing through various stages along this spiritual path. Bibi Rasti would often perch herself on a rock surrounded by large trees and focus on the remembrance of God. Bahu held his mother in such high esteem that on one occasion, he told her: *"You have been my teacher, and now you have become my spiritual guide."* Bibi Rasti replied: *"My son, I have given you all my prayers. You must look for a spiritual master."* Continuing: *"You cannot attain gnosis unless you have a master."* Sultan Bahu asked his mother for an indication of whom to seek, and she informed him: *"I smell your master from the East."*

If the Lord were found by bathing and washing,
He would be found by frogs and fish.

If the Lord were found by having long hair,
He would be found by sheep and goats.

If the Lord were found by staying awake all night,
He would be found by the cuckoo.

If the Lord were found by being celibate,
He would be found by gelded oxen.

The Lord is only found by those, Bahu,
whose intentions are good.

He did not remain at home for long afterwards, setting off towards the East searching for his master.

Early in his journey, Sultan Bahu was instructed by a local saint to go to Delhi to become a follower of Abdul Rahman Qadiri. At that time, it was the daily practice of Abdul Rahman to give guidance to his devotees. On this day, he mentioned to them: *"Today there is a special person who is coming to meet us. Go and greet him outside."* He gave a detailed description of this special person, so his devotees could recognise Sultan Bahu when he entered Delhi. When they did, he was immediately invited to meet Abdul Rahman. Upon their meeting, Abdul Rahman took hold of Sultan Bahu's hand. He brought him into his private chamber, where he initiated him into the Qadiriyya order. Since Sultan Bahu was already detached from dunya, his ascension on the spiritual path was nigh-on instantaneous.

He then sought to test out his newfound spiritual power. Later that day in the market, he focused on the Hindus and Sikhs passing within his gaze. His glance was so powerful that each and every one of them instantly became a Muslim. The devotees became aware of these antics and quickly reported Bahu's abuse of power to their master. The master was saddened to hear the news and he summoned Sultan Bahu to his chambers and asked of him: *"What is this, I hear?"* Sultan Bahu replied: *"Master, when a woman goes to the market to buy a utensil, she first tests it to see if it will last. If a boy goes to buy a bow or an arrow, he tests its flexibility. Master, you said you had given me spirituality, so I thought it was only right that I too test it."* Abdul Rahman smiled at the response, and his disappointment just as swiftly turned to happiness. From that moment, Sultan Bahu surrendered both his body and soul to his master.

When the word '*dunya*' is mentioned, the typical understanding shows its limitations so grossly that people's immediate response is to identify it, more often than not, as something material. Hence, dunya is commonly associated with the amount of wealth one may possess or is linked to a flagrant pride in one's family and children. However, some prophets and saints were surprisingly wealthy and were even married with children. However, they were always detached from dunya.

"The likeness of the life of this world (dunya) is that of water which We send down from the sky, which then mingles with the earth's plants to provide food for both people and animals. Then, when the earth is at its loveliest and takes on its fairest guise, and its people think they have it under their control, Our command comes upon it by night or day, and We reduce it to dried-out stubble, as though it had not been flourishing just the day before! Thus, do We make Our Signs plain for people who reflect." (10:24)

Dunya is an enigma that most people are never able to unravel. The fundamental illusion of dunya is that it does not exist by itself. Still, it is only formed by the forging of attachments. The truth is that only when people are attached to anything that takes them away from God's awareness, even for a moment, then that attachment becomes dunya.

"Know that the life of this world is mere diversion and play, glamour and mutual vainglory among you and rivalry for wealth and children—like rain, whose growth impresses the farmer. Then it withers and you see it turn yellow, then it becomes chaff. Whereas in the Hereafter there is forgiveness from God and His approval and a severe punishment. The life of this world is nothing but the wares of delusion." (57:20)

> *Seekers of this world are like dogs,*
> *wandering from door to door in wonder.*
>
> *Their attention is riveted on a bone,*
> *their lives wasted in bickering.*
>
> *Short on intelligence and unable to understand,*
> *they set out in search of water.*

Apart from the recollection of the Lord, Bahu,
all else is idle chatter.

Sultan Bahu lived in the world as if he were a traveller - enjoying the solitude and detaching people from the world's attractions.

In the beginning, when Adam took a bite of the apple, he immediately felt a need to relieve himself. Adam was, understandably, unsure of what to do since heaven had been a place of purity and sanctity. It would be unbefitting for the Garden to serve as the grounds for a lavatory. God thus ordered His angels to escort Adam to a place that would be appropriate – we call that place dunya. The Prophet ﷺ mentions that God had never created anything which He disliked more than dunya. On one occasion, the Prophet ﷺ went through the marketplace with people on both sides of him, and he passed by a dead body of a deformed sheep. He took the deformed sheep by its ear and then said to the crowd: *"Which of you would like to have this for a dirham?"* The people replied: *"We would not like to have it for anything. What would we do with it?"* He again asked the people: *"Would you like to have it?"* and they replied: *"By God, even if it were alive, it would be defective since it is deformed, and now it is dead."* The Prophet ﷺ said: *"By God, this world has less value with God than this animal has with you."*

It is for this reason that the Prophet ﷺ gave the following counsel: *"Do not let dunya eat away your faith like fire destroys wood."* Due to the love of dunya, people perceive sins to merely be tiny flies passing by their noses.

Half the curses on the world,
and all of them on the worldly

Whoever does not sow in the path of the Lord
will reap the lashes of torment

Burn, evil world,
which causes fathers to sacrifice their sons!

Those who give up on this world, Bahu,
will gain gardens of paradise

Religion and this world are blood sisters;
intellect did not teach you this

That both should be betrothed to one person;
the law does not permit this

Just like fire and water,
which cannot stay in one vessel

He is deprived of both worlds, Bahu,
who makes false oaths.

On the Day of Judgement, dunya will appear in the form of a hideous crone, showing no teeth, evil blue eyes, and a thin stomach. When people see this ugly crone, they will become frightened and exclaim to her: *"Who are you?"* They will then be told that this, indeed, is dunya. Then God will order the angels: *"Throw this old woman into hell!"* The crone will then speak and ask Him: *"My Lord, what about my lovers?"* At that point, God will say: *"All those who loved her, take them there as well."*

"The life of this world is nothing but diversion and play, but the abode of the Hereafter is indeed Life (itself), had they known!" (29:64)

Imam Rabbani warned: *"Association with the people of dunya is a slow poison. A sensible person will run away from such people. Such people do not only harm your body but destroy your faith. Do not even deign to look at their faces, for they will put you to sleep forever and strip you of your passion for God."* Association with such people is not the only poison dunya uses to pollute the intentions of those who aspire to connect with God. When people try to follow the right path and attempt to avoid the pitfalls of dunya, it responds by openly tempting people and brazenly offering itself to them. To completely detach from dunya and resist its temptations is impossible.

But those rare persons who do possess such a capacity are respected by dunya. They possess no feelings of greed for the material world and have, indeed, already attained spiritual death-in-life. Thus, dunya only wishes to serve them, as exemplified by the following incident:

It is said that Dunya once arrived at Abu Bakr's house, telling him: *"Please accept me. I have come to serve you."* Abu Bakr then rejected dunya, saying: *"What have I to do with you when the Prophet ﷺ did not accept you?"* Dunya then moped onto the house of Umar in search of acceptance, but this time she was met with a stick and beaten, then told to go away.

"Whoever is heedless for an instant is a disbeliever in an instant," so said my guide
My eyes opened to hearing these words, and I turned my attention to the Lord
I put my life in His trust; such is the love I gained
I died before dying, Bahu, only then did I find my purpose

Since the saints are the protectors of our faith, it is their eternal role to guide people's hearts away from dunya and usher them instead to the spiritual path. Such is the allure of dunya, the greed thus instilled within people always pollutes their intentions, even when they visit a saint. A disciple once visited Bu Ali Shah Qalandar and complained that his situation had worsened since he last visited. The master replied to him: *"O fool, the remembrance of God is like soap, and dunya is dirt; when you rub the soap, it cleans the dirt."*

"The love of [worldly] allures, including women and children, accumulated piles of gold and silver, horses of mark, livestock, and farms has been made to seem decorous to mankind. Those are the wares of the life of this world, but the goodness of one's ultimate destination lies near God." (3:14)

In the poetry of Sultan Bahu, as you would expect, one finds a constant reverence to his master:

The perfect guide thrashes one like a laundryman beats clothes
He purifies with his gaze, and he soaks one in bleach and soap.
He makes the dirty white and does not leave a speck of dirt
One should have such a guide, Bahu, living in every cell of one's being.

Having recognised the true minuscule value the physical world holds, it becomes necessary for the seeker to remove the shackles or remain forever imprisoned. Only the man of God can free the seeker from their attachment to the physical world.

Sultan Bahu spent all his life teaching and guiding people to the salvation of the spiritual world. He died in 1691 and was buried outside Shorkot. In 1775, the Chenab River changed its course and threatened to wash away his grave. To avert a disaster, Bahu's grave was dug up and moved to its present location. His shrine still functions as a site of pilgrimage for people from all over Pakistan. Radiating from his shrine and his voluminous poetry, he continues to offer guidance, support, and blessings to the faithful as he did throughout his lifetime.

The guide planted God's jasmine plant within me
He watered my veins with "negation and affirmation."
Blossoming, the bush spread its fragrance through me
Long live my perfect guide, Bahu, who has planted this shrub!

"*Apart from
the recollection of the
Lord, Bahu, all else
is idle chatter.*"

Sultan Bahu

The Fashioner

BEAUTY

Sayyid Isa Gilani (d.1781)

In 1990, I fell in love at first sight with Sayyid Isa Gilani when I visited his shrine in Istanbul. I was unable to uncover much information about him. However, that did not stop me from often name-dropping him as the epitome of spiritual beauty in my lessons. The article was compiled by Majid and Saheed in 2014.

'God is Beautiful and loves beauty' (Muslim)

One day, a young man - a mere novice on the spiritual path - stopped on the brink of a garden. He felt that the garden was beckoning him to enter. He did enter, and the garden felt tranquil. As he observed the picturesque beauty surrounding him, he contemplated how the garden illustrated man and nature's relationship so lushly. Suddenly, his eyes were fixed to a tree, under which sat a Darwish. His face was covered and seemed in meditation. The novice shook his head and thought to himself: *'What a foolish person. He has closed his eyes to a beauty that displays the true Glory of God.'* He walked up to the Darwish and told him: *"Open your eyes."* The Darwish paid no attention to the novice. He raised his voice and said again: *"Open your eyes and see the Glory of God!"* Again, the Darwish just ignored him, and the novice then shouted in anger: *"You are sat here in such a wonderful place. You should be busy appreciating the beauty of the garden!"*

Suddenly, the Darwish lifted the cloth away from his face and opened his eyes. The novice was startled by the Darwish's piercing gaze. The Darwish gently replied: *"My dear friend, why do not you close your eyes and see the Creator of this beauty?"* The novice was left speechless, and he sat on a nearby bench to contemplate this reversal. The Darwish's words and eyes had unsettled him. So, once again, he approached the Darwish: *"Excuse me, sir. I am sorry for being such an idiot. Could you please explain what you meant?"*

The Darwish told him: *"Go on your way, young man."* The novice pleaded: *"Please, sir, you have perturbed me. I cannot leave without an answer. We cannot attach physical attributes to His beauty, but how then can I appreciate God's beauty?"* The Darwish replied: *"We must realise that we know nothing about God's beauty. To gain an understanding of this matter, we need guidance from the awliya. Sayyid Isa Gilani - a Turkish mystic from the eighteenth century - had a profound understanding of the varieties of beauty. Holy people like Sayyid Isa are aware that all types of beauty stem from God. They emphasise to us that all of these manifestations are just a mere glimpse of God's beauty."*

The novice then thought that perhaps he had delved into matters that he could not comprehend. However, Sayyid Isa's name struck a chord, so he asked to know more about him.

The Darwish then narrated a tale concerning Sayyid Isa:

"In 1990, I travelled to Istanbul and was residing at a friend's house. It was a little after midnight when my friend suggested that we take the chance to visit the Sufi shrines. After we had already visited several, we came to a building at the top of a hill. As we entered the courtyard of (what I came to know was) Sayyid Isa's shrine, I smelt a beautiful fragrance. I noticed a Lotus tree to the side in full bloom. My friend plucked a flower from it and gave it to me. After paying our respects, we returned home. That night in a dream, I saw him - Sayyid Isa. Instantly, I was struck by his beauty. He was especially handsome, with a head of jet-black dreadlocks and a long

beard. *He wore a black turban and held a beautifully carved wooden walking stick.
In his other hand, he held a flower from the Lotus tree, which he also gave to me.
Ever since, when I mention beauty, the image of Sayyid Isa comes to mind."*

The novice was impressed by this account: *"Listening to you, I imagine that
Sayyid Isa must have been adorned with immense beauty. After our first meeting, I,
too, kept seeing your piercing eyes."* Shaking his head in disapproval, the Darwish
said: *"My young friend, I have committed to answering your questions, so there is
no need for flattery. In our society, we maintain a limited understanding of beauty.
The visual aspect of beauty attracts all the attention, be it the full moon, the rising
sun, or a scenic image. Sayyid Isa lived his life dedicated to the spiritual path, as he
was a pious and righteous man. By refining his inner beauty, this quality manifested
through his outward form. This is how the physical features of the awliya become
such a transparent reflection of their inner being."* The Darwish sensed by now
that the novice had a genuine interest in Sayyid Isa. So he granted him some
information about Sayyid Isa's background.

Sayyid Isa was a descendant of Shaykh Abdul Qadir Al-Jilani (1078–1166). In line
with his ancestor, he possessed immense physical and spiritual beauty. Sayyid
Isa belonged to the Qadiriyya order. He based himself in Istanbul's most well-
frequented area, surrounding Sultan Ayyub's shrine. Sayyid Isa was already
both the imam of the mosque and the shaykh of the lodge.

At this point, the Darwish became animated whilst speaking: *"You see! Showing
reverence to the Sayyids (descendants of the Prophet ﷺ) is an example of a beautiful
act in the Divine Presence. Through such an act, immense blessings are granted.
However, Islamic history shows us that not all people have shown the respect and
love due to the Sayyids. This was the situation during the Umayyad dynasty when
the descendants of the Prophet ﷺ faced persecution. The Sayyids wished only for a
peaceful life. However, some Umayyad rulers could not accept that the Sayyids were
so beloved by the masses. Some other rulers were blinded by petty jealousy and pride.
Thus, they thought they simply did not need any blessings from the Sayyids. After*

subsequent persecution, many Sayyids migrated to areas free from the influence of the Umayyads. Some families travelled to Persia, settling in an area in the north called Gilan (Jilan in Arabic). And in that time, it was common for families to be known by the name of their region."

Having listened attentively to the Darwish so far, the novice commented: *"A thought has just occurred to me. You mentioned pride. Was it due to this sin that some of the Umayyad rulers could not appreciate the beauty of the Sayyids?"* The Darwish nodded in approval. The novice began his own narration: *"The treatment of Sayyids by some Umayyad rulers contrasts that of the later Ottoman Sultans, who showed sheer reverence for them. This must be why the Ottoman Sultans were granted their seven-hundred years of rule by God; and why the Umayyad dynasty lasted less than a century."*

The Darwish smiled and replied: *"Well, it seems my words are not lost on you."* He then stood up and took out a small coin from his pocket before saying: *"Something as small as this coin can be an instrument to blind you."* The novice did not understand and said: *"Just when I thought I had fully understood you, you baffle me again."* The Darwish placed the coin in front of the novice's right eye and asked him: *"What do you see?"*

The novice remained silent. The Darwish waved the small coin: *"This is what people are obsessed with, and so, it blinds them."*

After a few moments of silence, the Darwish continued his screed on the many other acts that may prevent people from seeing God's beauty: *"The awliya warn us that the most destructive acts are ones that stem from arrogance and pride. Not even a glimpse of God's beauty is ever given to such people. Only when the heart frees itself from such vices are the eyes opened to notice beauty in every situation. It is for this reason that the Prophet ﷺ explicitly warned against pride, saying: 'A person with an atom's weight of pride in his heart would not enter Paradise.' The atom is, of course, millions of times smaller than the coin I was just holding."*

The Darwish then said: *"Know in your heart that it is not a sign of pride to dress well, but only when you look down upon people and deny the truth. Sayyid Isa's ancestor, Shaykh Abdul Qadir, wore glamourous clothes befitting a king. Once, he was questioned about his attire, and he pulled out the edge of his coarse undergarment. He quipped: 'The outer clothing is for you, and the inner garment is for God.'"*

It is still necessary for all those working for their Lord to maintain a high standard of beauty in their manners, conduct and appearance. There is such a command from God to the believers: *'O Sons of Adam! Take your adornment at every mosque...'* (7:31) This applies equally to our physical appearances and the spiritual side of our being. We can notice this maxim at work in the awliya, in particular, Sayyid Isa, who maintained a pleasant outer appearance. He understood that most human beings find it difficult to perceive beauty within their fellow men, as many only see the virtue's physical side. They do not naturally possess the ability to notice inner beauty.

The Darwish then discussed the perils of this superficial beauty desired by the ego: *"In society today, all that people are truly obsessed with is the physical beauty of other people. People do not know and do not want to know the difference between love and lust. I will share a tale with you to explain this point: once, a young man was instructed by his master to meditate in seclusion. The master also instructed a young lady to ensure that food was served daily for the young man. After a few days, she remarked to the master that the young man had become infatuated with her. The master gave the young lady a concoction that, upon drinking, resulted in her becoming catastrophically ill with diarrhoea. The master also instructed her to dispose of her excrement in a nearby bucket.*

Subsequently, whenever the young lady served the young man food, he no longer tried to gain her attention but began avoiding her. This was because her illness had caused her whole complexion to change. When the master was informed about the sudden change in the young man's attitude, he said to the lady: 'So the desire has gone, and now he avoids you. Now go and take that bucket and tell him, 'I am the same woman; all I have lost is the contents of this bucket. Have what you desired.'"

The Darwish then said to the novice: *"Nonetheless, do not think that physical beauty does not contain blessings. You have a handsome face, and such a beautiful feature is one you have been blessed with from God. What is detrimental in this context are the pathological obsessions with physical beauty that dominate our society, manufacturing a mountain of false perceptions. If we were to ask people on the street to name any beautiful person, they would surely mention a famous young celebrity. You will hardly ever find old people being mentioned. This is because we still fail to accept that there is a certain grace in growing old. However, the Prophet ﷺ has said that if a believer has grey hair, this is a sign of beauty marked by God. We should always remember that no matter how beautiful we may be in the present moment, we will all turn to indiscriminate dust one day. By following the Prophet's ﷺ teachings, we can improve our character and ultimately attain that inner beauty. This type does not fade away.*

One of the Prophet's ﷺ teachings concerns the three beauties that have the most soothing effects on the heart. He said that the first two types were the simple ones: looking intensely at the greenery and running water. Back when you mentioned you were attracted to this garden, you said it gave you a tranquil feeling. Such beauties always positively affect human beings, and many people are inevitably attracted to them.

However, suppose a group of people were to walk around this garden. In that case, some will notice certain beautiful details that others will ignore. This is because people need to fix themselves in a state of aesthetic appreciation to fully reveal themselves. People will come to this garden dozens of times and never have the experience you felt as you entered. Beauty hides from so many people."

The Darwish then mentioned the third type of beauty the Prophet ﷺ had spoken of – that is, to look at a beautiful human face: *"A beautiful face has many* features, the best of which is the smile. It is a truly infectious thing and has a sudden impact on others that cannot be ignored. And it is narrated by the Prophet's ﷺ Companions that they never saw anyone smile more than him.

Another special feature of a beautiful face is the eyes. The eyes cannot be missed as they are so directly appealing. Those who were fortunate enough to look at the face of Sayyid Isa would be left feeling intoxicated by his eyes alone. This was because he spent his time in remembrance of his Lord. He was granted a personal majesty in his eyes by God. This was so effective that when ordinary people glanced at him, they saw a glimpse of his entire being just in the eyes. People could not look into them for more than a few seconds as they could not absorb their power."

The Darwish then recited the following poem:

"The beautiful maiden, an epitome of beauty, is shy.
She hides from the gazes of people.
But the ugly beast goes around boasting he is handsome."

Having said this, the Darwish said to the novice: "Know, that real beauty tends to be hidden. We can see the most beautiful faces of the awliya, but we must be patient to see them. It will never be revealed to us prematurely."

The novice was keen to know about this supposedly hidden aspect of beauty. He was becoming accustomed to being left baffled by the Darwish's revelations and could not understand how this was possible. He was so far only aware of the five senses. The Darwish tapped the heart of the novice repeatedly and told him: "This is your sixth sense; this piece of flesh has eyes. The eye of the heart requires an endless effort for it just to open. It is not accessible to everyone, but when that eye does open, you see a beauty that the head's eyes never can.

Amongst the Prophet's ﷺ Companions, the heart of Abu Bakr was mostly praised by him. He proclaimed: 'Even the moon and the stars are proud of you, Abu Bakr, because of your beautiful heart.'"

The Darwish then narrated how the Prophet ﷺ would often praise his Companions for the immense beauty they possessed: *"And it is well known that prophet Yusuf was the most handsome of people amongst the prophets. Once, during a famine, his people were forced to survive without food for three months. He was instructed to stand on a raised platform in the centre of the town and shout to the masses to look at him. Once they saw Yusuf, the people became intoxicated, and the thought of food did not even enter their minds."*

Having listened to this incident, the novice then enquired about the beauty of the Prophet ﷺ. The Darwish responded: *"On this matter, the Prophet ﷺ has said, 'No one knows my reality except for God.'*

We have now reached the crux of the matter regarding the beauty of God. God addresses the Prophet ﷺ, saying: 'Had I not created you, I would not have created the universe. Were it not for you, I would not have created Adam. Were it not for you, I would not have created the universe.' So, we must be aware that the Prophet ﷺ intimately reflects the beauty of God. This reflection by itself contains more beauty than the whole of creation and everything contained in both realms. This is because the Prophet ﷺ is truly the first creation."

The Darwish conceded to mentioning some aspects of the Prophet's ﷺ beauty to the novice. But still, he warned, he must stay conscious that even the best descriptions of him could not reveal the true reality: *"Many of the Companions would often say they had never seen anyone like him before or after. Even they, his blessed Companions, were not capable of seeing and retaining his reality."*

The Darwish then related how Imam Qurtubi (1214–1273) once claimed: *'The Prophet's ﷺ full beauty has not been manifested; his absolute beauty was never shown. For if it was disclosed in full, then no one person would be capable of seeing it. Therefore, the examples that describe his beauty are no more than the briefest glimpse of his actual reality.'"*

The Darwish then related remarks from the Companions of the Prophet ﷺ

regarding his beauty:

"These traditions describe the Prophet ﷺ as the epitome of beauty. His beautiful face is compared to the full moon, glowing and luminous. Those blessed by God to see him mention that their hearts would be put at ease instantaneously. When he would speak, it was as if a radiant light emitted from his teeth. The words of Anas are indeed appropriate: 'The Prophet ﷺ was the most beautiful of God's creation.'

The great Sufi master, Imam-i- Rabbani, once remarked that his biggest regret in life was that he was not born in the Prophet's ﷺ time. Even though he had an extremely high rank in his own right, this misfortune still caused him much pain. However, these feelings vanished whenever he sat with his master, Khwaja Baqi Billah (1563–1603). The reason for this is that the awliya exist to absorb aspects of the Prophet's ﷺ beauty. No one can understand his full beauty, but its aspects are still somewhat apparent amongst the awliya. The awliya encourage us to follow the Prophet's ﷺ characteristics and adapt them so that we too attract such aspects of this perfected beauty."

The Darwish finally mentioned to the novice that it was now time to conclude their conversation. He told him: *"Remember these words of advice - the Prophet ﷺ once said, 'When you ask someone for help, ask from a beautiful face.' By now, you should know that he is not alluding to beauty's physical aspects but advising you to seek help from those who possess both inner and outer beauty. This greater combined aspect of beauty is always apparent within the awliya - those pious people like Sayyid Isa.*

We have often been instructed to say: 'O God, You have made my appearance beautiful, now make my character beautiful.' We should instead be aware of the purpose of our creation. God created us for beauty; now, our own responsibility is to ensure our character becomes beautiful.

To fulfil this duty, the Prophet ﷺ advises us to adopt the characteristics of God. Sayyid Isa was a prime example of a friend of God and manifested himself through such characteristics. He was not attracted to physical beauty but lived his life in the constant presence of God. He was rewarded with a Divine dress that, even now as we speak, makes him even more beautiful."

These were the final words between the two. The Darwish and the novice embraced and then, after reading *Fatiha* for Sayyid Isa, departed.

"God is Beautiful and He loves beauty."

Prophet Muhammad ﷺ

The Praiseworthy

DHIKR OF THE HEART

Hafiz Muhammad Hayat (1839–1916)

Hafiz Muhammad Hayat was the grandmaster of Hadrat Sahib and was often mentioned by him. I visited his shrine and met many of his pious descendants, who actually live in the UK.

A devotee once went to visit his master, who enquired of him: *"There is a mystic, Sain Nur, who resides in your area. Have you ever met him?"* The devotee replied that he did his best to avoid him, as he often seemed on the brink of madness. The master, undeterred, said: *"You should go and meet him and give him my greeting."* So, the devotee went to meet Sain Nur. As soon as Sain Nur noticed the devotee, he announced to his company: *"He is the one who has been criticising me!"* Suddenly, Sain Nur ordered all his other visitors to leave. He then instructed the devotee to enter. He then asked him: *"What if a person makes a profit of twenty-four thousand per day? What if a person makes a loss of twenty-four thousand per day?"* But it seemed as if Sain Nur was talking to himself. He did not explain what the phrase had meant, then he suddenly left the room, leaving the devotee puzzled.

The devotee returned to his master and narrated the entire incident. The master merely commented: *"What wise words Sain Nur has spoken."* The master noticed the confusion now etched on his devotee's face. He explained: *'Sain Nur gave you the example of the number of breaths a person takes daily. If you remember God every day twenty-four thousand times, you are rich. And if you do not remember God, you lose twenty-four thousand times a day, so you are, in truth, a beggar."* The devotee wondered how it could be possible to remember God in every breath. He could not imagine such examples as the Naqshbandiyya order - renowned for their emphasis on guarding every breath. 'Hosh dar dam' (awareness in the breath) is their major principle, and it is their practice to remain attentive in every breath. Shah Naqshband states: *"The foundation of progress on this path rests on the breath."*

In a small fishing village on the modern-day border of Pakistan and Kashmir, there once lived a renowned spiritual master, Hafiz Muhammad Hayat. More specifically, he was born near Jhelum. He dedicated his entire life to teaching people that the heart's true purpose was to always be conscious of God. His father, Muhammad Bahadur, was a pious person who had decided to keep his spiritual state hidden from people. Hafiz Muhammad Hayat's early education was local. It was his practice from childhood to remain quiet and isolated instead of playing with other children. He often went alone into the forest, and, from a very early age, he developed an immense passion for the Qur'an. He began to memorise it and his passion was such that at night he continued studying whilst all others slept. He would even tie his long hair to the ceiling to ensure he stayed awake.

To complete his memorisation process, he travelled to Dina, a nearby town. His teacher, Hafiz Khwajuddin, taught him to recite the Qur'an in the Hijaz dialect - the way the Prophet ﷺ recited it. His recitation was reportedly so beautiful that, during Ramadan, many learned people came to pray behind him. Under his teacher's guidance, Hafiz Muhammad Hayat involved himself in one of the most effective dhikr methods by reading, understanding, and reflecting on God's words. For example, in one verse, God states: *"O you who believe, remember God with much remembrance"* (33:41). God makes a direct command in this verse, which obliges the believer to remember God always. Ibn Kathir

(1300–1373) states: *"Hajj takes place at a specific place and time. Fasting and prayers have a beginning and an end time."* He then explains that the one form of worship for which God has set no boundaries is dhikr. Al-Qushayri adds: *"There is no fixed time for dhikr. The most honourable worship is prayer. And though it is not permissible to read at certain times, dhikr is permissible at all times."* Hafiz Khwajuddin quickly realised that Hafiz Muhammad Hayat had immense spiritual potential. Thus, he felt the need to take him to a living spiritual master.

So, one day, Hafiz Khwajuddin took Hafiz Muhammad Hayat to Bawali Sharif. He was initiated by Khwaja Muhammad Bakhsh into the Naqshbandiyya Mujaddidiyya order, and his master granted him permission to open a madrasa to teach people the Qur'an in his village. Hafiz Muhammad Hayat began to teach the Qur'an. Once, two of his former students were taken to another teacher. After listening to their recitation, the teacher immediately sent them away and said: *"Take them back to their first teacher, Hafiz Muhammad Hayat. The way they recite the Qur'an is marvellous. No one else in our region can recite the Qur'an in the Hijaz dialect."*

On another occasion, a visiting imam overheard the recitations of Muhammad Hayat's students. He came to ask Hafiz Muhammad Hayat if he could be convinced to come to his area and teach his children. Hafiz Muhammad Hayat declined and told him: *"Many students come from far and wide to study here. If I were to move out, it would become impossible for them to find me."* Due to his innate integrity, Hafiz Muhammad Hayat never asked for funds for the madrasa. He laboured most of the day as a farmer. His uncle soon realised that his nephew showed an unparalleled dedication and passion for teaching. So, he chose to donate some of his own land for the accommodation of students.

Once, two people came and sought spiritual guidance from Muhammad Hayat. Thus far, he had not officially initiated anyone into the spiritual path. So he said to them: *"I will need to take you to my master in Bawali Sharif."* He found out that his master was busy visiting his devotees in a nearby village when he arrived there. He continued his journey to the nearby village, and when his master finally saw him, he beamed with delight. After greeting his master, Hafiz Muhammad Hayat mentioned to him: *"Master, these two people want initiation, so I have brought them to you."* *"But it is up to you to initiate them into the path,"* replied his master.

A message was delivered to Hafiz Muhammad Hayat from a local saint, Pir Sayyid Neyk Alam Shah (d.1899), from Mirpur. Consequently, Hafiz Muhammad Hayat met Pir Neyk Alam, who told him: *"We have a special Mujaddidi connection, and we have been looking for a capable person to carry it for a long time. We believe you are that person."* Following this, Hafiz Muhammad Hayat then visited both Bawali Sharif and Pir Neyk Alam. Whenever he went to sleep, he would ensure that his feet were not in the direction of these two places nor towards the madrasa he had studied at. One day, he received another message from Pir Neyk Alam that he must visit Imam-i- Rabbani's shrine in Sirhind. He then spent three days and nights in Sirhind and received countless blessings.

The Prophet ﷺ mentioned the three dimensions of faith - *"Iman, Islam, Ihsan,"* beliefs, actions, and sincerity. In line with all the great masters and Sufi writers, Imam-e Rabbani regarded Sufism as Islam's innermost aspect and the best servant of Shariah. Thus viewing themselves as the servants of the Shariah, the Naqshbandiyya masters base all of their teachings on the Qur'an and the Sunnah. And so, this was Muhammad Hayat's practice too. Once, he is said to have stopped at a mosque during his travels along with some devotees. During the prayer, the mosque still remained empty. So he sent two of his devotees to ask the local people if anyone would come to the mosque to pray. When the devotees spoke to the local people, the people replied: *"We have a mosque. However, we do not know how to pray."* When Hafiz Muhammad Hayat was informed of the situation, he was greatly saddened and said: *"We must stay here and teach them."* And hence, he then sojourned a few days in the area to teach the local people how to pray.

The Naqshbandiyya are also renowned for their emphasis on dhikr and consider it one of the greatest forms of worship. Dhikr is of two 'types' - with the tongue and with the heart. A man once came to the Prophet ﷺ and told him: "*O Messenger of God* ﷺ, *the laws and conditions of Islam have become too numerous for me. Tell me one rule that I can always keep to.*" The Prophet ﷺ replied: "*Always keep your tongue moist with the remembrance of God.*" Aishah narrates further: "*The Prophet* ﷺ *said: 'God favours silent dhikr above loud dhikr seventy-fold. On the Day of Resurrection, God will bring human beings to His account. The recording angels will dig out what they have written, and God will say: 'See if something that belongs to my servant was left out?' The angels will reply: 'We left nothing out concerning what we have learnt and recorded, except that we have assessed it and written it.' God will then say: "O My servant, I have something good of yours for which I alone will reward you - your hidden remembrance of Me.*'"

Mullah Ali Qari (d.1606) states that: "*It is not possible to keep up the dhikr of the tongue all the time as it is not permitted in certain circumstances. This is only possible with the dhikr of the heart.*" In certain situations, it is not permitted to make dhikr of the tongue, like when one has the need for the call of nature. The Naqshbandiyya masters explain that doing dhikr of the heart without ever raising one's voice is better than any loud dhikr since God states: "*Do bring your Lord to remembrance in your very soul, with humility and in reverence, without loudness in words, in the mornings and evening, and be not of those who are unheedful.*" (7:205)

The Naqshbandiyya masters also mention that to follow the direct command that God has made upon the believers - that is, to make abundant dhikr - is only possible with the dhikr of the heart. Aishah mentions that the Prophet ﷺ once prayed the sunnah prayers for Fajr and then laid down until she could hear him snore. Afterwards, she said to him: "*O Messenger of God* ﷺ, *you fell asleep. I could hear you snore.*" The Prophet ﷺ replied: "*O Aishah, my eyes sleep, but my heart does not.*" The Naqshbandiyya masters make such a point of emphasising the heart's dhikr because the heart is the abode of God. The true purpose of the heart is to beat in His remembrance. The Prophet ﷺ says: *"In a person, there is a lump of flesh, and if it is kept wholesome, the whole body remains in a healthy condition. If it is corrupted, the whole body is ruined. This lump is the heart."*

The attachment to the physical world is, as mentioned, the major impediment preventing the attainment of any form of spirituality. The seeker on the spiritual path is usually made aware by his master that the two most harmful enemies he must conquer are the ego and the material world. It is also necessary for him to continuously strive to subdue the ego, purify his heart and rid himself of its desires so that his being turns fully towards God. By practising the dhikr of the tongue, a person can then begin to try the dhikr of the heart. A devotee once mentioned to Shaykh Abu Uthman: *"Master, when I remember God, I find no sweetness in my heart."* He replied: *"Praise God that at least one of your limbs is mentioning Him."* Therefore, a person should be thankful that remembrance is at least on the tongue, so we can persevere to achieve the heart's dhikr. Both types of dhikr have their own benefits, but the most powerful progress is achieved through the heart's dhikr. It magically reduces one's love for the world and cripples the distractions of the ego.

One day, Khawaja Abdul Khaliq (1044–1179) was studying with his teacher when he came upon the following verse: *"Call unto your Sustainer humbly, and in the secrecy of your hearts. Verily, He loves not those who transgress the bounds of what is right."* (7:55) The words prompted him to ask his teacher, Shaykh Sadruddin: *"Teacher, what is the meaning of this verse? How can one perform dhikr in the heart? If one performs audible dhikr people can hear you. But if one performs the silent dhikr, then Satan is aware of it. The Prophet ﷺ mentioned that 'Satan moves freely in the veins and arteries of the sons of Adam.'"* Shaykh Sadruddin replied: *"My son, this is a hidden knowledge. I hope that God puts you in touch with one of His friends. He will teach you the reality of secret dhikr."* Khwaja Abdul Khaliq then lived in suspense, awaiting the friend of God who would teach him these divine mysteries. And one day, he met with Khidr, who taught him the dhikr of the heart.

Mullah Ali Qari mentions that the Naqshbandiyya masters emphasise the silent dhikr. This maxim is based on the following hadith: *"The best dhikr is the silent dhikr, and the best provision is what suffices."* The Prophet ﷺ said: *"The dhikr not heard by the recording angels equals seventy times the one they do hear."* Hence the dhikr of the heart is a far more precious thing for remaining hidden. God says: *"I am to My servant as he expects of Me, I am with him when he remembers Me. If he remembers Me in his heart, I remember him to Myself. If he remembers Me in an assembly, I mention him in an assembly better than his."* (Hadith Qudsi). The reward for loud dhikr in a gathering is that God remembers that person in the gathering of angels. The honour God gives to a person who remembers Him through the heart is a little different. The virtue of a silent dhikr is that the person is personally blessed with God remembering Him alone. There are many different types of dhikr and the Naqshbandiyya emphasise the dhikr of 'Allah'. Anas narrated that the Prophet ﷺ said: *"The Last Day will not come until 'Allah, Allah' is no longer said upon the earth."*

In the Naqshbandiyya path, as we have described, the devotee does dhikr of God twenty-five thousand times a day. For this, it is necessary to close the mind to everything extraneous. So it is necessary to clear the mind of distractions to focus. It is recommended that the devotee focuses on their master before they perform the dhikr. One must sit on one's knees as in the position of prayer. One should fold the left arm over the stomach and the right arm over the left, signifying the ego's control. The head is then tilted down towards the left nipple where the spiritual heart is located - two fingers below the nipple, to be precise. The seeker closes his eyes, visualising at that moment that he is closing all the channels of distraction. His tongue is then raised and stuck to his palate, and his teeth are locked together to close his mouth. The seeker then imagines that the heart itself is black, and the word 'Allah' is written in white on the heart.

Then the seeker focuses on the heart and begins his remembrance alone, saying 'Allah' in the heart. As the seeker focuses on the sweetness of remembrance within the heart, his breath is restrained below the navel. The seeker continues to breathe only through his nose.

Shah Naqshband recommends that devotees also read the following supplication so that the heart can attain contentment: *"O God, You are my purpose, and Your pleasure is my goal. Grant me Your love and Your awareness."* Since this is the beginning of the remembrance in the heart, it is necessary to persist until the heart is fully awake. The above prayer merely helps the heart to focus. The devotee who achieves success can then perform silent dhikr in any situation. Every step could be dhikr if the focus stays on the heart even whilst walking down the street. Hadrat Sahib advised the Sangis: *"Whatever situation you are in, all you need to do is imagine the image of the word 'Allah' in your mind, and that will help you to focus."*

Once, Khwaja Muhammad Baqi Billah (1563–1603) made this request of his master: *"I wish to meet the Qutb of the time."* His master gave him permission to travel to Srinagar in Kashmir. Upon arrival, Khwaja Muhammad Baqi Billah was surprised that the person whom his master had named as the Qutb, was in fact, a guitar-maker. Khwaja Muhammad Baqi Billah watched him stretching strings and realised that the job required a lot of precision. He thought: *"If he needs to pay so much attention to his job, how does he ever find the time to remember God?"* When the Qutb had finished his shift, Khwaja Muhammad Baqi Billah greeted him with respect and said: *"When my master sent me to you, he mentioned that you are not heedless of God for the blink of an eye. I confess I am a foolish person, but please explain to me how you make dhikr and keep your inner state alive whilst you go about this work?"*

The Qutb explained: *"This is our way - we must be forever occupied with some trade, but meanwhile our hearts must be busy with Him. In truth, my heart never moves away from God, not even for a split-second."* At that moment, the Qutb taught Khwaja Muhammad Baqi Billah about the concept of silent dhikr – how the greatest ambition was to make the heart stop on God so that each breath is taken in His awareness.

Meanwhile, following in the footsteps of the Naqshbandiyya masters, Hafiz Muhammad Hayat spent the better part of his time occupied in worship, teaching the Qur'an and summoning dhikr gatherings. Throughout all these activities, he remained in the state of silent dhikr. Those around him remained unaware of this. To comprehend this dhikr's spiritual nature, the reader should recall the incident of the devotee and Sain Nur at the beginning of this chapter. On one occasion, Hafiz Muhammad Hayat spent the night at a mosque in a village and engaged in silent dhikr of the breath whilst he slept. The next day, some village women spoke amongst themselves, saying: *"Last night, there must have been some Jinns in our mosque, because all night we could hear heavy breathing noises coming from the mosque."*

Hafiz Muhammad Hayat held an immense love and respect for his own spiritual masters and contemporaries. He honed loyal friendships with other spiritual masters of the region, including Miyan Muhammad Bakhsh (1830–1907) and Qadi Sultan Mahmud. The respect these masters had for each other was always evident; whenever they would reunite, each would say to the other: *'You lead the prayer.'* One day, Hafiz Muhammad Hayat sent the following brief to Qadi Sultan Mahmud: *"I wish to meet you once more."* When Qadi Sultan Mahmud read this message, he began to cry, and as he stared into an empty space, he said: *"God willing, we will meet in such a month."* Qadi Sultan Mahmud made arrangements to set off. When he reached Kharri Sharif, he said to his devotees: *"Hafiz Muhammad Hayat is coming – make proper preparations so he can rest."* The devotees of Qadi Sultan Mahmud were surprised. No one had previously mentioned to them that Hafiz Muhammad Hayat was coming on that day. Later, Qadi Sultan Mahmud added: *"If Hafiz Muhammad Hayat is alone, invite him in here."* A private meeting then took place between these masters, following which

Hafiz Muhammad Hayat commented: *"Before I had met Qadi Sultan Mahmud, I had no strength and was so weak. After I met him, my pain was taken away."* This was the last meeting between the two friends, as Hafiz Muhammad Hayat suddenly became extremely ill.

However, despite his illness, he still offered his prayers with the congregation. One day, a Sangi visited Hafiz Muhammad Hayat and asked him: *"Master, how is your health?"* Hafiz Muhammad Hayat replied: *"I will inform you in two or three days."* This was an indication, lamentably, that he only had a few days left to live. He read the Islamic creed the last time and died at sunrise. The funeral was held the next day. It was not possible to inform people more than a few miles away. But suddenly, Qadi Sultan Mahmud arrived anyway. Hafiz Muhammad Hayat's widow was bamboozled: *"To what do we owe this honour?"* she asked. He replied: *"I have come to read the funeral of Hafiz Muhammad Hayat."*

The local scholar and saint Mawlana Muhammad Abdullah (d.1960) gave a memorable, emotional eulogy. Every attendee cried. Another scholar, Mawlana Muhammad Ibrahim, hosted the funeral itself and stated in closing: *"I was worried about leading the mourning of such a holy person, but I am privileged to have been given this honour."* Hafiz Muhammad Hayat was buried in Dangrot, which later became submerged. To save his memory, his body was relocated to its present-day shrine near Chaksawari in Azad Kashmir.

"Call upon your Lord humbly and secretly. Surely, He does not like the transgressors."

The Holy Qur'an [7:55]

The Supreme Bestower

FULFILLING THE
NEEDS OF PEOPLE

Sidi Bel Abbas (1129–1204)

I was not aware of Sidi Bel Abbas before I visited Marrakech in 2009. After that, his shrine became a default pilgrimage on our numerous visits to Morocco. I bought an Arabic book on his life and learned the facts of the following chapter.

Within the narrow alleys of the old town of Marrakech, you may find the famed *'souks'* - the largest marketplaces in Morocco. They are a vast amalgamation of vibrant colour and energy, and, as you enter, they seem to transport you to another age; to some exotic place of intrigue and adventure. The air is rife with the cries of gypsies, while the pavements are filled with snake charmers, magicians and folksingers. Strolling further through this maze, it may seem as if nothing is sold here, judging by what you overhear of the haggling between buyers and sellers. Though this scene may seem like an overwhelming parade, unbeknownst to ordinary tourists, such theatrics are not the only deals taking place in the souk.

Within the heart of the old city is situated a spot that can be easily missed. A small door is all that distinguishes it from its neighbouring stalls. This door leads to a retreat away from the hustle and bustle of the souks. This space is a haven for those unlucky souls who seek support and assistance. Within the confines of a courtyard, a congregation of people sit attentively on benches with their backs slumped against the wall. One's first impression is that of a waiting room in a doctor's surgery. It is quickly apparent that some amongst the company are blind or disabled. They all sit patiently, waiting to be summoned, but no one is employed to summon them. This is no doctor's surgery, and none of them have booked appointments. Venturing further inside the complex, you will find a special room that houses the saints' tombs of old. The current congregation has come today to seek support from just one of them: the patron of this complex, Sidi Bel Abbas. Despite their fears and traumas, these people have a total assurance that Sidi Bel Abbas will indeed hear their pleas and come to their aid.

Abu Ayyub Al-Ansari was once seen crying at the sacred chamber of the Prophet ﷺ. He was asked why he was doing this, and he replied: *"I am not crying to brick and mortar! This is my Prophet! I have a need - he will solve it."* With such conviction, people flock to the graves of Sidi Bel Abbas and his fellow saints. Known as courts in the sub-continent, the people visiting these places do so in the manner they would envisage themselves arriving at the saint's living court. Here, their present-day case will be presented before the compassionate saint, who will undoubtedly call his judgement in their favour. Knowing full well that they can always seek a saint's help and support from the relative comfort of their homes, many of them still make the arduous journeys to such holy spaces with the hope that sheer proximity to the awliya will speed up the process of grace.

In his own lifetime, Sidi Bel Abbas was already a source of comfort and support to many. And even after hundreds of years, he can still fulfil the needs of his people. His full name was Ahmad Ibn Ja'far Al-Khazraji, and he was born in Sabta, Morocco. He was given the kunya, Abu Al-Abbas. His surname suggests that his lineage traces back to the Ansar (local people) of Madinah. He was affectionately known as Sidi Bel Abbas and is recognised as one of the seven patron saints of Marrakech. Noticing Sidi Bel Abbas in a cheerful mood, one day, a student seized what he thought was an opportune moment to ask him about his personal life: *"Tell me about how all this began, master. How did all this happen to you?"* Sidi Bel Abbas calmly responded: *"I became an orphan at an early age, and my family's circumstances were such that I was sent to work with merchants. However, I had no interest in trading and money matters. Instead, I was inclined towards a spiritual master, Shaykh Al-Fakhariji - a renowned student of Qadi Iyad. Shaykh Al-Fakhariji taught a lesson in the local area, and I became a regular attendee. However, this impacted my livelihood, which enraged my mother. My family was extremely poor and in need of my earnings to provide for their basic needs, and so, out of despair, she beat me. I stopped attending the lesson and went back to working full time with the merchants. To my surprise, a few days later, Shaykh Al-Fakhariji visited me, asking why I was no longer attending his class. I informed him that I wanted to come and listen to his teachings, but, alas, my circumstances could no longer allow it. The shaykh listened attentively and then immediately went to visit my mother. He informed her that he would take it upon himself to financially support my family and cover my tuition fees. And indeed, from that day on, Shaykh Al-Fakhariji ensured that the needs of my family were met, and he provided the means for me to study."*

During this period, Sidi Bel Abbas completed his memorisation of the Qur'an, studied Maliki fiqh and received higher education from his spiritual master, Shaykh Al-Fakhariji. Sidi Bel Abbas went on: *"It was during my studies that the following verse of the Qur'an kept recurring in my thoughts - "Verily, God orders you to be just and benevolent"* (16:90). *I kept on reciting this verse, and I realised there must be a deeper meaning, as God is commanding us to do two deeds: to be just and to be benevolent. I found the answer to this quandary when I later read that the Prophet ﷺ instructed the Ansar brothers to give half of their wealth to the migrant brothers. I now understood that this was the meaning of being just - to learn to give away half of what you have."*

"Then I further studied the biography of the Prophet n. Many moral examples were mentioned in which the Companions gave away everything they possessed. So I felt that this verse had revealed the purpose of my life. I made a firm intention to ensure I performed both deeds as part of my actions. So I started to provide for the needs of eighty-three people; including my immediate family, many poor relatives, students, and some poor families in the local area. I also sponsored thirty-two orphans. If any of these individuals no longer needed my support, I replaced them with another needy person. I did this for sixteen years, and my life revolved around justice and benevolence. In return, God rewarded me with the authority to appoint rulers and have them removed at my discretion. Other great matters were also freely handed over to me."

The student, needless to say, was captivated by this detailed account. However, Sidi Bel Abbas did not then elaborate on the true nature of his spiritual rank. Nonetheless, the student understood this to be the sign that he was the Qutb (the *'spiritual pole'*). The same student then recalled an incident to him: *"I remember when we once travelled through a certain area, and you instructed a wealthy person in that region to give charity to the local people. This wealthy person arrogantly commented that God did not require his wealth. We were instructed to write down a date, and you said to us that this foolish person had just lost his position. Twenty-three days later - the exact day we wrote down - this wealthy person was removed from his position."* In response, Sidi Bel Abbas recited the following verse from the Qur'an: *"God is Self-Sufficient, while you are the needy"* (47:38). Like that very same wealthy person whom Sidi Bel Abbas chastised, it has become disappointingly common for us to overlook a simple fact about our natural disposition as human beings. This self-deception has left us unaware that we are always in 'need'. This ignorance is due to our current selfish outlook on the living of life. It is also based on our foolish presumption that a poor person and a needy person are basically the same ilk. We do not recognise the distinct difference between the two. We cannot understand how God Himself has defined humanity. Irrespective of our worldly status and wealth, we are all needy. All human beings, rich or poor, need oxygen with every breath. They live in need of food and sleep and shelter and love and so on. Realising for ourselves that God does not need anything and becoming aware of our basic shared state as human beings force us to consider: *'Who do we turn to in our neediness?'*

Our first instinct is to think that we must just make supplications to God, and our needs will be fulfilled. However, whilst we do so, we must still follow the methods of Sidi Bel Abbas, who, throughout his lifetime, contemplated myriad questions and kept a routine of always looking for answers in the Qur'an, the Sunnah, and the various teachings of pious people. The Prophet ﷺ says: *"Amongst God's creation, there are those whom God created to fulfil the needs of others. Hence, people shall seek their help."* It is common knowledge that the role of Jibril was to bring revelations to prophets. Not so apparent is that his key role is spelt out as *'the fulfiller of needs.'* Each day, all the millions of supplications made throughout the world are first received by Jibril. Accordingly, he chooses which ones to immediately pass up to God and which can wait. People's needs are then summarily fulfilled by God's special servants that He has placed on every continent. Whenever sincere supplications are made by the common people, these servants become obliged to see such needs fulfilled. These servants live among us, and their lives do not revolve around themselves. They have followed the Prophet's ﷺ instructions and have adorned themselves with God's qualities - such as generosity, compassion, and personal charity towards people in need. All they truly seek is God's pleasure, as they realise that their purpose is to help God's creation, as God loves those who are considerate towards His creation. These qualities are most apparent in the awliya, the special servants, like Sidi Bel Abbas, who become the *'fulfillers of needs.'*

During his early life, Sidi Bel Abbas was based in Agadir. Being a mathematician of a high-calibre, he taught students who stayed at the city hotel. Whatever he was paid for his teaching, he would immediately spend it on food from the market to feed the students and poor people in the vicinity. One day, some young students at the hotel were threatened with execution by the king's royal guards, as they had raised their voices during the middle of the night whilst debating an incidental matter. The students were all frightened at the prospect of being beheaded, understandably. They swiftly flew to Sidi Bel Abbas, knowing that he could and would help them in their moment of need.

Sidi Bel Abbas was always concerned about such unlucky souls and thoroughly disliked the arrogant and the unjust. After hearing the students' account of their stakes, he went away into his private chambers for a long while. Upon returning, he told them: *"I pleaded to God; you are all safe. But those guards will not see another day. They will be executed for threatening those who study the knowledge of the Prophet ﷺ."* The students pleaded that this seemed too drastic a response. Sidi Bel Abbas shrugged: *"If you do not want them dead, then they will receive a hundred lashes for making these threats."* Later, the guards were arrested due to a bottle of wine being found in their vicinity. And indeed, they received the fixed punishment for drinking alcohol in that era - a hundred lashes.

Ibn Rushd (1126–1198) once instructed his many friends to visit Marrakech to sit in Sidi Bel Abbas' congregation. When one of his friends returned, Ibn Rushd asked him: *"What is the way of the master?"* His friend replied: *"His path is just to fulfil the needs of other people. Even when he has a clear need himself, you can see him giving preference to others. He was extremely handsome, always wore a cloak made from wool, and often went around the streets reprimanding people for missing the prayer, not giving generously to charity, and not following the Shariah. His humility is such that he practices the concept of self-blame, hiding his inner state, often speaking in riddles. I never witnessed any backbiting in his gatherings. The essence of his teaching is based on pure benevolence. He teaches that you will only attain when you give to others and that a person should live through benevolence. He explained to us that such a state of being means just to desire for others what you desire for yourself."*

Sidi Bel Abbas always encouraged people to perform the best of actions, giving charitably. He promoted this concept because he believed it would steer people away from the worst of actions – that is, to be miserly. Sidi Bel Abbas explained that such is our need. If God were to withhold His generosity from us even for one moment, we would perish. Therefore, we should not withhold ourselves from being generous towards people, as God Himself is always the arch-provider and can fulfil people's needs in other, unforeseen ways. He provides us with the opportunity to be generous towards His creation, so we should not disappoint Him.

In every situation, we can find the means of being generous; either by using our wealth or being considerate towards one another or even just speaking kind words with our tongues. As this insight does not often enter our minds, we seldom seek opportunities to serve God's creation. This way, we remain oblivious to the divine blessings we would be granted if we practised generosity in every situation. Unlike the common people, the awliya possess generous souls. They are always mindful that God is the ultimate provider for His creation in every matter. They always keep an eye out for people in need. If no one comes to them seeking assistance, they feel that God must be upset because they have not been presented with new chances to serve Him. The Prophet ﷺ, as mentioned, explains how God bestows certain special individuals with the function of being the 'fulfiller of needs'. Following this role, God always obliges them to come to the aid of all needy people, even if they are totally unknown to them.

One day, Sidi Bel Abbas caught a cold, and so his family buried him in blankets. However, he still lay shivering. Suddenly, he threw the blankets off and walked out into the streets. As he looked around, he came across a family who had lit a fire in a dark corner and were shivering just as badly. Sidi Bel Abbas understood immediately that this family was the reason God had not let him rest. So he went back home and arranged food and bedding for them.

In the classic work, Risala Qushariyya, Qushayri (986–1074) comments that an essential quality for those embarking on the spiritual path is tawakkul - reliance upon God. God Himself says: *"And whoever so puts his trust in God, He shall suffice for him."* Sidi Bel Abbas adds further: *"As a young man, I heard the sayings of many pious people on this concept of tawakkul. I reflected upon it. I concluded that I had to abandon my attachments to all worldly matters and possessions to hold complete trust in God. I quickly abandoned everything and set off into the wilderness. Later that night, as I rested in a mosque, I overheard a commotion. A cow was missing, and the owner and his friend were busy searching for it. The search had brought them to the mosque. They noticed me, and I mentioned to them that I was a traveller. They carried on with their search, but a few moments later, the cow's owner returned with food, bread, and milk. He then invited me to come and stay at his house. When we reached his house, the missing cow was there. The owner realised that the cow was never missing in the first place. This situation had ultimately occurred to allow him to look after me, as I was a traveller who was relying on God."*

It is a common situation for the awliya to retreat like this into the wilderness to practice tawakkul. They plan only according to God's pleasure and to challenge their inner self - not over a quick matter of days, but year after year. The only period in our life where tawakkul is actually truly practised is in our infancy. Then we are totally reliant upon our mothers. We remain oblivious of achieving this state; whenever we are faced with inescapable dilemmas; our reliance is not on God but on certain people or authorities within society. To the awliya, having such a petty form of reliance constitutes shirk ('idolatry'), as God has set this condition for His believers: *"Put your trust in God if you are truly believers"* (5:23). Sidi Bel Abbas taught this concept a little more subtly: *"Tawakkul is when the only plan you have is God's pleasure."*

One particular student, Musa Ibn Hamad, had attended Sidi Bel Abbas' gatherings for many years but could not quite figure out his teacher's reality. Musa relates: *"One day, we had just finished praying Fajr in the mosque. It was Arafat day, and Sidi Bel Abbas instructed me to give away everything I had on my* person to the first person who entered the city gate. Or else, he said, I should go away. An old lady walked through the gate, so I freely gave her all the money I had. After this, Sidi Bel Abbas raised his hand, made a supplication, and we offered prayers. Sidi Bel Abbas then commented that we had combined two things of great merit - charity and prayers. At this moment, I underwent a spiritual experience that had an immense and enduring impact on me. By living through this incident, I became aware that Sidi Bel Abbas was clearly instructing me to practice tawakkul."

On another date, it had not rained for a long time in Marrakech. Musa asked Sidi Bel Abbas why he had done nothing to alleviate the people's suffering. Sidi Bel Abbas replied: "Just as you are withholding, God also withholds." Musa was accustomed by now to hearing his teacher speak in riddles, and he understood then that no charity had been given. Thus, God was withholding the rain. Sidi Bel Abbas then stated the following hadith: "O son of Adam, you spend, and I will send." Musa obediently gave charity and, soon after, rain fell once more across Marrakech. This incident became well-known in the community, and people quickly became mindful of Sidi Bel Abbas' spiritual rank.

On another day, Sidi Bel Abbas found himself sitting in a friend's shop when a poor person approached them and repeatedly asked for coins with which to buy food. Sidi Bel Abbas apologised, as he did not have any money, and then he turned to his friend and asked him to give the poor man some money to buy bread. After the poor man left, Sidi Bel Abbas said to his friend: "I sense you're worried about how I will pay you back. You have failed to realise that this poor person has just saved you from the burden of poverty. Such is the favour God has given you for fulfilling this poor person's needs." In such ways, Sidi Bel Abbas helped people in need throughout his life. He was always aware that the Prophet ﷺ had said: "If anyone fulfils his brother's needs, then God will fulfil his needs." The awliya, like Sidi Bel Abbas, seek to please the Prophet ﷺ by sincerely following his teachings.

Abdul Rahman was a man who did not have a good opinion of Sidi Bel Abbas.

However, on one night, he saw the Prophet ﷺ in a dream and asked of him: *"What is your opinion of Sidi Bel Abbas?"* The Prophet ﷺ smiled, replying: *"He is amongst the ones who will cross the Bridge by lightning on the Day of Judgment. This is the category of the chosen people."*

*"If anyone fulfills
the needs of his brother
then God will fulfill
his needs."*

The Prophet Muhammad

The Honourer

SALAWAT

Sain Tawakkul Shah (1839–1897)

In the 1970's, I happened to read a detailed biography of Sain Tawakkul Shah, and I have quoted his wisdom ever since. He is a wonderful personality, and I still gain great pleasure every time I read about him.

The importance of giving blessings unto the Prophet ﷺ is illustrated by the following narration by Imam Qushayri (986–1074): *"On the Day of Judgement, one believer's sins will outweigh his good deeds. At that moment, a person will come and place a piece of paper, which will increase the tally of good deeds such that they outweigh the sins. He will say, 'May my mother and father be sacrificed for you. Who are you?' The person will then reply, 'I am your Prophet, and this piece of paper is the salawat you have read upon me. I have come to help you in your hour of need!'"*

One fine day, many centuries ago, the Companions of the most beloved of creation were sitting amongst themselves in the sacred sanctum that is the Prophet's ﷺ mosque. The Prophet ﷺ then entered the masjid, to the apparent delight of the Companions. They marvelled at the Prophet's ﷺ blessed face, which seemed to them more luminous than ever. Furthermore, news of glad tidings was obviously forthcoming, judging by his expressions. They remained silent and eagerly awaited his speech. Sensing their excitement, the Prophet ﷺ

spoke: *"Jibril came to me and delivered this message from God - 'Are you not happy, O Muhammad, that whenever someone sends blessings upon you once, I shall send ten blessings upon him. If one person from your nation sends one salutation upon you, I will reward him by giving ten blessings in return."*

The value of sending blessings upon God's most beloved is also revealed to us through the following narration by Ubay Ibn Ka'b, who once asked the Prophet ﷺ: *"O Messenger of God ﷺ, how much of my supplication should I devote to you?' He replied: 'As you desire'. I said, 'A quarter of it?' He said, 'As you wish, but if you were to increase upon this, it would be better for you.' I said, 'Half of it?' He said, 'As you like, but if you were to increase upon this, it would be better for you.' I said, 'Two-thirds of it?' He said again, 'As you wish, but if you were to increase upon this, it would be better for you.' Finally, I said, 'And if I dedicate my supplication in its entirety to you?' He said, 'Then your needs will be satisfied, and your sins are forgiven."*

God grants such rewards for sending salawat, as it is an act that He also does Himself. He mentions in the Qur'an: *"God and His Angels send blessings on the Prophet. O you who believe, send your blessings on him, and salute him a thorough salutation"* (33:56). As this is an act done by God, it is an act that never ceases and can never cease. We can also safely assume that God has always bestowed blessings on the Prophet ﷺ. The first depiction of love in the history of creation is this love and bond between God and the Prophet ﷺ. It is not possible to define this love - it is an unimaginable and unquantifiable love. As such, it is an obligation given to every believer to send blessings on the Prophet ﷺ. To read salawat is thus to fulfil God's command and, by doing so, to express our love towards the Prophet ﷺ. This act of sending salawat has been a practice of all the prophets of our faith, reaching all the way back to Adam's blessings when he sought to marry Hawa. The angels said that he must give a dowry and when Adam asked them how he was to do this, the angels replied: *"Send salutations upon the Prophet ﷺ three times."* Whilst in paradise, Adam gave his son Sheth the following advice: *"Remember that, after our Creator, God, the most special being in existence is the Prophet ﷺ. I base this truth on my personal experience. I have seen the name of the Prophet ﷺ set next to the name of God - whether it was written on the leaves of the trees, emblazoned on the fruits, inscribed across the chests of the houris or carved on the throne of God. It was everywhere, therefore show him honour."* This advice that Adam gave to his son was meant to help him understand that there is no real separation between God and the Prophet ﷺ. To remember and love the Prophet ﷺ is the same as to remember and love God. The Muslims do not directly worship the Prophet ﷺ, yet still, they consider obedience to him a form of submission to God. The following incident helps us to reflect upon the uniqueness of this relationship. Once, a Companion erred and sought forgiveness. He went to the Prophet's ﷺ mosque and tied himself to a column. He declared that he would not move from the spot until God had forgiven him. He remained there for some time before the Prophet ﷺ heard about his oath. The Prophet ﷺ then quipped: *"Had he come to me and sought forgiveness, surely he would have been forgiven, but he has gone to God directly, so that is a matter between him and God."*

Sain Tawakkul Shah was renowned in his own day for his near-excessive love of the Prophet ﷺ. Physically, he was of medium height, had a broad chest and bore strong features. He had long hair that reached his earlobes, and he had a full beard. His eyebrows were thin, like twin crescents, and his forehead was wide. His eyes were big and bright and always beamed with the love of the Prophet ﷺ. He had a fair complexion and rosy cheeks. One of his followers, Mahbub Alam, narrates of him: *"One day, I was sitting with another follower, and the shaykh was asleep. We had a hand-fan, and we used it to keep the shaykh cool. Later, when I looked closely, I could not see whether the shaykh was breathing. I kept looking for a further ten minutes, but I could not see any bodily movement. I turned to my friend and panicked that the shaykh was not breathing. As we were talking, Sain Tawakkul Shah awoke and asked what the matter was. We mentioned how we were worried about the shaykh. He looked at us and responded: 'This is because I was in Madinah.' I immediately thought that he must mean he had just seen Madinah in a dream. Sain Tawakkul Shah looked at me and corrected my thoughts: 'No! I was in Madinah. There are men of God who, if they lift their eyes and then look down, at that moment they can be in Madinah and back.' And as he said this, both my friend and I were just as suddenly transported to Madinah and back in a glance."*

Sain Tawakkul Shah[1] was born in 1839 in Punjab, India. He was, at first, an only child and then became an orphan at an early age. Thankfully, his grandfather was linked to the Qadiriyya order and was made responsible for his upbringing. From the start, Sain Tawakkul Shah loved to meet holy people, and as a young boy, he made every effort to sit in their company. This was the main reason that, while still a youth, he departed his home and went to Ajmer. There he met a Chishti shaykh, with whom he spent most of his time. This shaykh's practise was to go into seclusion after Fajr prayers and then remain there until midday. The shaykh also declined to participate in the qawwali gatherings. Eventually, the local people pleaded with Sain Tawakkul Shah to ask the shaykh to join them in the qawwali gathering. He mentioned this request to the shaykh soon afterwards, who responded: *"Son, they will not be able to bear the intensity of my love."* However, Sain Tawakkul Shah persisted, and the shaykh finally conceded to attending the gathering. After a short while amongst his devotees, the shaykh became so intoxicated that he shouted out, *"Illallah!"* And as a result, all the people fainted. The shaykh made his way back to his chamber and said to Sain Tawakkul Shah: *"Son, I told you that they would not be able to bear my love."*

From here, Sain Tawakkul Shah picks up his own story: *"During my stay in Ajmer, I noticed that there was a lot of light and blessings being bestowed on the grave of Khwaja Gharib Nawaz (1143–1236). In one of my visions at the time, I witnessed a gathering of awliya, and each one was sat carefully at his place. I looked around, and I saw no space for me, so I jumped around like a child until I saw the leader of*

---

1 To be accurate, this is not his original name but a title bestowed upon him by God.

the gathering, Khwaja Gharib Nawaz. So I went and sat next to him. Many awliya did not approve of my behaviour, but Khwaja Gharib Nawaz said: 'Let him be. This boy is just intoxicated.'" In another vision, Khwaja Gharib Nawaz explained to Sain Tawakkul Shah that he belonged to the Naqshbandiyya Mujaddidiyya order and would find his true master in Punjab. So, as instructed, Sain Tawakkul Shah travelled back to Punjab. Along the way, he met a similarly intoxicated person who told him to go to a particular village. There he met an intoxicated woman, who remarked: "So you have arrived? Go, as the sun of guidance is about to set, quickly and take your portion." So he then continued until he reached the threshold of the master, Khwaja Qadir Bakhsh. The master asked, plainly: "Little by little or all at once?" Sain Tawakkul Shah replied: "All at once." So the master hugged him tightly and transferred to him so much spiritual energy in one moment that he became overwhelmed and fainted. One of the devotees who witnessed this commented: "He has become intoxicated! How will the order continue through him?" Khwaja Qadir Bakhsh heard this and replied, "The order will become far more widespread through his efforts, and my soul will nourish his devotees."

Sain Tawakkul Shah had true reverence for his master. In the circle of dhikr, he sat farthest from the master. However, he undoubtedly benefited the most. He lived in a perpetual state of simultaneous hope and fear during his time with the master. Whenever he heeded the call of nature, he would walk for two miles barefooted out of the village. When the master's son noticed this, he offered to make a hut for him nearby. Still, Sain Tawakkul Shah declined, saying: "How could I attend to the call of nature or even wear shoes in the vicinity in which my master resides?" After Sain Tawakkul Shah had served his master faithfully for a few months, he was instructed to go to Ambala. From Ambala, he occasionally returned to visit his master. He remarked in this time: "Spiritual appointment comes from the heavens as a gift from God. When this humble servant received permission to turn towards the spiritual path, I watched a turban suspended from the sky started wrapping itself around my head." When Khwaja Qadir Bakhsh died, some of his children were still quite young. So Sain Tawakkul Shah quickly took it upon himself to look after the family's welfare. He laboured on the farms and cared for the children by picking them up and playing with them joyfully. He relates how: *"Once, I was carrying a very heavy bundle of grass and had one of the master's sons around my waist. As I approached the house, the door was too narrow, so I carefully put the boy on the floor and took the grass through the door with great difficulty. The boy was upset and said, 'Take the grass back out. I want you to carry the grass and me at the same time, and only then will I be pleased with you.' So I carried out his request with even more hardship."*

Sain Tawakkul Shah lived a truly ascetic life without possessions or comforts. He slept on the floor because, in his view: *"When the master of both worlds, our Prophet ﷺ, slept on the floor, how can we ever sleep in luxury?"* Whenever people flocked to him seeking initiation, he would remark to them: *"You people are better than I - you pray, and you are pious, learned people. I am merely an ignorant person. It would be better for you to find someone learned to guide you."* Though some may have been deterred, others would persist until he belatedly relented and granted them initiation. He would then pray for them so: *"O God, You sent them to me, and I put my trust in You and teach them Your name, and I hand them over to You."* He did not like it whenever anyone stood up to show him respect. If someone started reciting poetry in his honour, he would become sad and say: *"I am not worthy of this praise, I am nothing."* His humbleness and detachment were plainly clear for all to see. He once announced: *"Only out of honour to the Sunnah of the Prophet ﷺ, do I approach my wife. Otherwise, even if the maidens from heaven were to come before me, I would have no interest.'*

Sain Tawakkul Shah loved to eat the foods that the Prophet ﷺ is said to have eaten. For breakfast, he would sometimes have egg, honey, and black-seed oil. He would change clothes on Friday, put kohl in his eyes and use perfume, as such are Sunnah acts. He ate lentils for dinner and rarely ate meat. He never complained about food and ate whatever was made for him. If anyone complained about a meal in his presence, he would tell them: *"Do not eat for two days, and then you will not be complaining."* Sain Tawakkul Shah was, by nature, the epitome of generosity. He never refused a beggar and always gave away whatever he came to possess. He never let anyone leave his home without eating. If it were not the time for food, he would send them away with some money for a meal. All of his visitors were treated equally, whether rich or poor, Muslim or non-Muslim, acquaintance or stranger. When his neighbour, an untouchable, died, Sain Tawakkul Shah did not eat until his body was cremated. He commented that it was just not befitting to eat whilst his neighbour's family was in mourning. His habits were such that if someone praised something he was wearing, he would donate it to them. Once, somebody bought a beautiful coat for him, and a devotee said: *"It looks very nice on you."* He immediately took it off and told the devotee: *"You keep it."* Out of sheer compassion, he never accepted any offerings from orphans. A woman once offered him some money, and he asked her: *"Is this the orphans' money?"* She replied, *"No, this is my own".* He said to her: *"Spend it on the orphans."* Once, he gave food to a Darwish, hoping he would give it to the birds, but the Darwish ate the food himself, thinking it was meant for him. Sain Tawakkul Shah became worried, and the Darwish soon realised his mistake and asked him forgiveness for his actions. Sain Tawakkul Shah said: *"You have eaten the right of the birds, so ask them for forgiveness."* The Darwish then gave all his ensuing food to the birds. When Sain Tawakkul Shah recited salawat, birds would come and sit on his shoulders.

One day, he joined a discussion regarding life and death. One person commented: *"It is often said that the Prophet ﷺ is alive, but we know too that he has passed away and is buried in Madinah. In what sense is he then alive?"* Sain Tawakkul Shah explained: *"He is alive in the sense that just as he had power and authority in his physical existence, he has that power and authority now. What he was able to do then, he can still do now."* Once, the Prophet ﷺ was asked whether the blessings sent upon him by people from afar would reach him, even after death. The Prophet ﷺ replied, *'I personally hear the salawat read by people of love. The other kind is presented to me as a gift by the angels. Either way, it is presented to me.'* Salawat that is heard by the Prophet ﷺ is accepted and acknowledged by him personally. Khwaja Qutbuddin Kaki (1173–1235) sent three hundred salawat on the Prophet ﷺ every night. After his second marriage, he began to neglect this practice. And so the Prophet ﷺ came to him in a dream and asked: *"Qutbuddin, where is your salawat? I have not received it."*

Sain Tawakkul Shah once explained that the Qur'an commands us that reverence and honour be shown to the Prophet ﷺ. One way of showing this reverence and honour is simply by sending blessings upon him. Sain Tawakkul Shah celebrated Mawlid on the 12th of Rabi Al-Awwal each year. He would sit in silent meditation at a distance from the gathering. Once, his devotee Sayyid Zahuruddin asked him: *"Master, why do not you sit in the gathering?"* Sain Tawakkul Shah replied: *"So much of the light of the Prophet ﷺ has descended on the gathering that I can barely remain conscious."* Sain Tawakkul Shah later related that, due to his constantly reciting salawat, he was blessed by the Prophet's ﷺ soul. He narrates how: *"In the beginning, I saw an image of a person who was extremely handsome, beaming with radiant eyes, wearing a turban with one tail. This image stayed with me. I was mystified as to whom the person was, and I did not mention it to anyone. Then, later, I started seeing two people. The second one had a turban with two tails. And these images stayed with me for a long time. Later, I found out that the first person was Shaykh Abdul Qadir (1078–1166) and that the second was the Prophet ﷺ. Then these images disappeared from my dreams, and I began to see the Prophet ﷺ whilst in a wakeful state, and my soul became lost in him. I enjoyed this state immensely."*

Sayyid Zahuruddin relates that Sain Tawakkul Shah once mentioned: *"When I recite the salawat, the soul of the Prophet ﷺ meets me and puts a garland around my neck."* Sain Tawakkul Shah also touched on how, when a person occupies himself with worship, he is faced with numerous trials and tribulations. However, the beauty of salawat is that a person is soon protected from all of these. He explained how every type of worship could be rejected due to some annoying fault or other, apart from salawat, which is never rejected. Whilst there is no minimum or maximum amount of salawat that should be recited, the recommended dose is to read salawat eleven hundred times daily. One of the benefits of reading salawat is that it enhances spiritual progress, as it awakens the inner self. Sain Tawakkul Shah remarked that a Sufi who remains truly consistent at repeating a particular litany would continue it even after his death. It is also related that Sain Tawakkul Shah used to lick his lips during certain litanies. When asked why, he would reply: *"When I read salawat or even the name of God, it feels like somebody is putting sweets into my mouth."* Towards the end of his life, Sain Tawakkul Shah suffered from a debilitating illness. And yet, he continued to pray with the congregation to his dying day. He remained occupied in reciting salawat upon the Prophet ﷺ. When asked to nominate a successor, Sain Tawakkul Shah said: *"My name is Tawakkul Shah, I have planted the seeds of trust upon God, and He will take care of it."* On the matter of his death, Sain Tawakkul Shah merely said: *"I saw my spirit wearing a green turban, and I saw the spirits of the awliya descend from the heavens and shake hands with me. I had a vision in which the imam of our mosque hugged me and told me, 'Shah Ji, they are waiting for you upstairs.'"*

"When I read salawat or even the name of God, it feels like somebody is putting sweets into my mouth."

Sain Tawakkul Shah

الفتّاح

The Supreme Solver

UNLOCKING THE HEART

Diwan Ali (d.1943)

Diwan Ali was not a renowned figure. Today, he is hardly known outside the circle of Hadrat Sahib's (1921–2008) followers. However, I have visited his simple grave in his remote village, and I felt his story was important and should be told. Afdal and Saheed compiled the original article in 2013.

During the early Makkan period of Islam, perhaps no one was more opposed to the new faith than Umar Ibn Al-Khattab (584–634). He openly rejected the Muslims and distrusted their departure from the traditions of their ancestors. Though of noble character and a man of integrity, he severely punished his people for converting to Islam. Irrespective of his intolerance, though, he somehow caught the Prophet's ﷺ attention, who began to mention him in his prayers: '*O God! Strengthen Islam by Umar Ibn Al-Khattab or Amr Ibn Hashim (Abu Jahl).*' The Companions found this prayer a little surprising since they knew both men to be staunch unbelievers.

Eventually, though, Umar became curious about the Prophet's ﷺ teachings. One day he covertly followed the Prophet ﷺ to his secret meeting place. However, his footsteps were soon heard by the Prophet ﷺ. Without turning around, he asked: "*Who's there?*" Umar quickly hid from sight. Although the Prophet ﷺ never caught him, he soon tired of the paltry measures of his surveillance. Umar then decided to put an end to the matter of Islam once and for all. Along the road one day, he met a person who asked him why he seemed so upset. He replied, plainly: *"I am going to kill Muhammad."* The person retorted: *"You had better first set your own house in order. Both your sister and brother-in-law have accepted Islam."* Hearing this, Umar flew into a rage and turned his steps towards his sister's house. When he arrived, he found the door of the house bolted from the inside. Both husband and wife were busy receiving lessons on the Qur'an from Khabbab. He knocked at the door and shouted for his sister to open it. Hearing Umar's voice, Khabbab hid in an inner room, forgetting to take the pages of the Qur'an with him.

When the sister opened the door, Umar struck her on the head, saying: *"You have renounced your religion."* He then went inside and inquired: *"What were you doing? Have you too forsaken the creed of our forefathers and gone over to the new religion?"* The brother-in-law interjected: *"What if the new religion is better and on the path of truth?"* Umar was enraged by this and quickly struck him too. When the sister intervened, he hit her on the face, and she started to bleed. She shouted: *"Umar, we are determined to live and die as Muslims, do whatever you like."*

When Umar's anger subsided, he felt the shame of having struck his sister. His eyes then fell on the pages of the Qur'an left behind by Khabbab. He said to his sister: *"Show me these pages."* *"No,"* replied the sister, *"You are unclean and cannot touch the Qur'an."* Umar washed his body and then took his chance to read the pages: *"Verily, I am God: there is no God but I: so serve Me (only) and establish regular prayer for My remembrance."* (20:14) The fear of God then gripped his heart, and the prayers of the Prophet ﷺ came to fruition. He wept and declared at that moment: *"Surely this is the word of God! I bear witness that Muhammad is the Messenger of God."*

Throughout our history, Umar's conversion story has captivated Muslims and non-Muslims alike. Perhaps that is why it has been dramatised multiple times as a serial on Arab television channels. He was the staunchest of the unbelievers, and yet, slowly, he was coming closer to an inevitable fate. Though his denials increased in intensity outwardly, internally, he was being broken down bit by bit. It is precisely this part of the story that appeals to the subconscious - the inward journey of an unwitting believer. The Prophet ﷺ mentions a lump of flesh in the body, which, if medically sound, implies that the whole body is healthy. However, if that lump of flesh is compromised, the whole body is also corrupt. That lump of flesh is the heart. In his state of unbelief, Umar's heart was locked, and so he rejected the truth. The Prophet ﷺ unlocked his heart. This inward journey had transformed Umar - from a stone-hearted person to one who would wander the streets at night seeking to help anyone in need. Just as the Prophet ﷺ unlocked the heart of Umar, the pious people have continued this tradition to this very day.

In recent times Qibla Alam (1870–1934) undertook this noble endeavour and unlocked many hearts. One, in particular, was of Diwan Ali, the tax collector of an area named Kulla in Kotli, Azad Kashmir. Qibla Alam's practice was to visit Kulla because his deputy, Miyan Fadl Ilahi, resided there. Qibla Alam normally stayed in the local mosque on each visit. However, if this proved impossible, then he stayed at someone's house. He was not in the habit of giving long speeches and preferred to teach the fundamentals of Islam. He used the anecdotes of the pious people to educate the simple farmers of the region. His sincerity was enough to pierce the hearts of his audiences.

On one occasion, Miyan Fadl Ilahi invited Diwan Ali to meet Qibla Alam. However, Diwan Ali was more interested in worldly matters. He pointed to his heart and said: *"This is locked, so what would be the purpose of meeting your shaykh?"* Diwan Ali's heart was locked because he had a notoriously volatile temper. Added to this, his position as a tax collector gave him all the arrogance of his profession. Qibla Alam began to focus on Diwan Ali's heart.

The role of the awliya is to unlock the hearts of people. We face difficulties in life primarily because our hearts do not function properly, and, in that poor state, we make wrong choices. The Prophet ﷺ states: *"The indication that God is unhappy with a servant is that the individual is preoccupied with useless activity. If an hour of a man's life slips by in another purpose than that he was created for, he will regret it. Additionally, if a person reaches the age of forty and his goodness does not overwhelm his badness; he should prepare himself for hellfire."*

The parable of the heart is then like that of a house with multiple doors. The point is to be careful and not allow anything harmful to enter through one of these doors, or the home will be ruined. The heart is the house, and the many doors represent the many potential sins. The seeker must be careful to not allow any such illnesses to enter. If these were to settle on the heart, this would only aid in locking the heart even tighter. Ibn Al-Mubarak says: *"I have seen wrong actions killing hearts. The heart's degradation may lead to it becoming addicted. Turning away from wrong actions gives it back its life. Opposing the self is the best action for it. Whoever is concerned with his heart's health and life, if he makes any mistake, he should hasten to wipe out its effects by seeking forgiveness from God."*

The Prophet ﷺ says further: *"A strong man is not he who defeats his adversary by wrestling, but a strong man is he who controls himself at the time of anger."* Anger is a slippery path – a person overtaken by this state has no control over his tongue or actions. In a fit of rage, he might curse his family or even physically assault them. In some ways, it could be best described as a state of intoxication. The person is similarly completely unconscious of his actions. At this point, the heart and the brain no longer function properly. The Prophet ﷺ says: *"Anyone who can control his anger, God will hide his faults."*

Additionally, he ﷺ goes on to say: *"The faith of a servant is not put right until his heart is put right and his heart is not put right until his tongue is put right."* Abu Bakr, following this advice, would place stones in his mouth to avoid speaking. Uthman says: *"A person slips more with his tongue than he does with his feet."* When entering Islam, the tongue proclaims the shahada. Hence, from a state of disbelief, the person becomes Muslim and inevitably closer to God. However, when the same tongue utters disbelief it takes him away from God. Suppose a person utters divorce to his wife. In that case, the relationship is no more, irrespective of how much love and affection previously existed between them. There is no turning back – the arrow has been shot and cannot be pulled back into the bow. The tongue is extremely dangerous, and many have slipped into the abyss just by its unwitting utterances. Qibla Alam always used a Farsi poem to illustrate the importance of controlling the tongue: *'Silence is better, even if you speak in pearls.'* The Prophet ﷺ says: *"Whoever can guarantee (the chastity of) what is between his jaws and what is between his legs, I guarantee him the Garden."*

The image of what one sees is imprinted in one's heart. This tendency can result in several kinds of corruption in the heart of a servant. The Prophet ﷺ said: *"The glance is a poisoned arrow of the devil. Whoever lowers his gaze for God, He will bestow upon him a refreshing sweetness, which he will find lodged in his heart on the day that he meets Him."* The devil enters through a glance, for he travels with it faster than the wind blowing through an empty place. He makes what appears more beautiful than it really is, and he transforms it into an idol for the heart to worship. He promises false rewards, igniting the fire of desires within. This distracts the heart and makes it abandon more important concerns. It stands as a barrier to reality, and so the heart loses its straight path and falls into the erroneous pit of desire and ignorance.

The consumption of small amounts of food guarantees the heart's tenderness, strengthens the intellect and one's humility, weakens desires, and enhances the gentleness of one's temperament. Overeating brings about just the opposite of all these praiseworthy qualities. It causes the body to incline towards disobedience to God and makes worship and obedience seem laborious. A full stomach and excessive eating make one sluggish and lead to disobedience and neglect of worship. Whoever safeguards against the evil of overfilling their stomach prevents greater evils from coming into the world. It is easier for the devil to control a person who has filled his stomach. The Prophet ﷺ said: *"Restrict the pathways of the devil by fasting."*

Rumi (1207–1273) says: *"The Lord lives in every heart. So, if you desire to win His pleasure, do not break anyone's heart."* Of all the ills and vices that could lead to the locking of one's heart, it is, in fact, the breaking of someone else's heart; that is considered the worst action. By doing this, you automatically risk locking your own heart and throwing away the key. Bulleh Shah (1680–1757) says: *"Destroy a mosque, or a temple, but do not break a heart."* Just as pleasing a heart is a beloved action to God - the opposite is true of breaking a heart.

Acts of obedience are essential to the heart's well-being as food and drink are indispensable to the body. All sinful actions are similar to poisonous foods that inevitably harm the heart. To maintain the health of the body, you should carefully follow a strict diet. Indeed, you must habitually eat good food at regular intervals. You must be quick to free the stomach of harmful elements if the wrong food is eaten by mistake. Of course, the well-being of the heart is far more important than that of the body. The well-being of the body enables man to lead a life free from the illnesses of this world. A steady heart ensures both a good life in this world and eternal bliss in the next.

As such, while the body's death may cut the servant off from the virtues of this world, the heart's death results in everlasting anguish. A righteous man once said: *"How odd that some people mourn for the one whose body has died but never mourn for the one whose heart has died - and yet the death of the heart is far more serious!"* Thus, acts of obedience are indispensable to the well-being of the heart. The following acts of obedience are the nutritious foods of the servant's heart: dhikr, recitation of the Qur'an, seeking God's forgiveness and invoking salawat (benediction) on the Prophet ﷺ. *"Verily! Only in the remembrance of God do hearts find peace."* (13:28). The principal effect of dhikr is to bring the heart back to the awareness of God. And so, various forms of dhikr can achieve this reconnection. These are silent dhikr, loud dhikr and the recitation of the Qur'an. To recite the Qur'an is the greatest of all dhikrs, and many people have come to Islam just by reading it. Supplication is the most honourable act of worship in the sight of God. The Prophet ﷺ says: *"There is nothing more honourable in the sight of God than supplication."* When speaking about the Prophet ﷺ, Rumi says he is like a magnet, and mankind is like metal – the stronger the connection, the closer one is drawn to the magnet. So, the more a person sends blessings upon the Prophet ﷺ, the stronger his link to the Prophet ﷺ becomes. And, without a doubt, the Prophet ﷺ will open their heart – with just one glance, he could unlock the hearts of his entire nation.

Rumi states: *"You have to keep breaking your heart until it opens."* Suppose you find yourself unable to unlock the heart through the conventional avenues of reading, praying and sending salawat. In that case, there are always alternatives, though not ones meant for the faint-hearted. However, suppose a person's heart is locked and impenetrable – though it may appear intact – it is, in fact, a useless tool. The role of the master here is to smash the heart to pieces so that it becomes alive. When you try and join the pieces together again, it finally begins to function. This process is as painful as it sounds but greatly beneficial. Allama Iqbal states in this regard: *"The heart is like a mirror. Do not prevent it from being broken. Its broken pieces are even dearer in the sight of God."* Unlike a mirror that loses value upon breaking, the heart gains value in God's sight the further it shatters into pieces. Just as a king destroys all in his path after conquering a city to make his imprint. God, likewise, wants to stamp His mark on the shattered remains of His followers' hearts. There are so many examples of this in the lives of holy people. The death of a dear friend or a woman's rejection spurs them to leave everything and solely devote their lives to God.

Once Diwan Ali had become a devotee and was steadfast on the spiritual path, Qibla Alam asked him if he regretted anything in life. He replied that his one regret was that God had blessed him with numerous daughters, but he still did not have a son. Even though Diwan Ali was in his sixties, Qibla Alam reassured him that God would belatedly grant him a son. He then advised him to marry his late brother's widow, Mai Kalu, already in her mid-fifties. When she heard of this proposal, she was (understandably) shocked and queried Qibla Alam: *"Can an old tree bear fruit?"* She decided to flee to the adjacent village, hoping that she could make her return when Qibla Alam had left. The thought of marrying her late husband's brother was too much to bear. Qibla Alam, however, prolonged his stay in the hope of personally formalising this marriage. Messages were relayed back and forth between the villages, but Mai Kalu would not relent. She felt her late husband had done nothing but trick her for all their time together. She could not now bring herself to marry the equally temperamental Diwan Ali. Even after desperate reassurances from Qibla Alam that they were bound to share a good and blessed marriage, she remained unconvinced. Qibla Alam then invited her to meet with him, and she accepted. Qibla Alam told her: *"We have been waiting for you for fifteen days. Please accept our proposal. If you do so, then God will bless you in both worlds."* She eventually consented and was married to Diwan Ali. Her acceptance pleased Qibla Alam, who then blessed her in return. When Qibla Alam left the village and stated that he would return once they had received the blessing of a son. Sometime later, miraculously, Mai Kalu assuaged Diwan Ali's only regret.

Hadrat Sahib narrates further: *"Once, I visited Diwan Ali's home with Qibla Alam. He presented Qibla Alam with an incredibly beautiful buffalo in honour of the visit, but he refused. Diwan Ali folded his hands and humbly informed Qibla Alam, 'By not accepting this gift, you have only increased this wretched person's misfortune.' Seeing his state of despair, Qibla Alam was finally obliged to accept it. This buffalo remained at Checheyan for many years."*

Hadrat Sahib continues in this vein: *"I stayed at his house on numerous occasions. After Qibla Alam's demise, my main reason for going to Kulla was to visit Faujdar Khan (d.1960), who was posted at a nearby customs checkpoint. Diwan Ali was a close friend of Faujdar Khan, and apart from being sangis, both were deputies of Qibla Alam. Later in life, Diwan Ali was granted official permission to guide people to God. Transforming from an arrogant man to a humble human being, Diwan Ali exemplified the process of unlocking the heart."*

Once, Diwan Ali requested of Hadrat Sahib that he wanted to kiss the soles of his feet, as he was the son of his master Qibla Alam. Hadrat Sahib was shocked by this request and humbly declined the offer. Diwan Ali died on 18th April 1943 in Kulla, his ancestral village, and was buried near his house.

"If you want to soften your heart, feed the poor and pat the head of the orphan."

The Prophet Muhammad

الغفّار

The Great Forgiver

SELF-BLAME

Dhul Nun Al-Misri (796–859)

Shaykh Dhul Nun is a classical Sufi master who is mentioned within major Sufi works. I read about him in many books; however, I could not visit his shrine when I visited Cairo in 2011. After that trip, I saw him in a dream, and a strong bond was established between us. I made the intention to pay my respects to him on my next visit, which I did. Nasir and Saheed compiled this article in 2017.

A Darwish once boarded a wooden boat that was ferrying passengers across the river Nile. He quickly found a corner where he could sit quietly and meditate without being disturbed. Amongst the passengers was a rich jewel merchant. He had hidden his gems in the seams and folds of his clothes. He would often feel out these hidden gems just in case one had gone missing. To his alarm, one did somehow go missing during the journey. He frantically searched everywhere but could not locate his priceless gem. One by one, the passengers were taken aside and searched by the merchant and his servants. Finally, they all reached the unanimous conclusion that the jewel must be with the Darwish. His appearance showed signs of poverty, and the fact that he had remained silent throughout the journey was deemed adequate proof of his guilt. They set themselves on him like wild hyenas, treating him with total disrespect. He endured their treatment patiently, and in his heart, he proclaimed: *"O, God, You know the reality of this matter!"* At that very moment, thousands of fish raised their heads above the water, each bearing a jewel in its mouth. The Darwish leaned out of the boat, carefully took one jewel from one fish, and gave it to the merchant. All onboard fell at his feet and begged his pardon for the disrespect they had shown him earlier. This was not the Darwish's way - he had no desire to reveal his true state or gain any following amongst men. Before the passengers could say any more, he leapt from the boat and swiftly walked across the surface of the river Nile and disappeared. The passengers were even more astonished, and stories about this Darwish spread swiftly across Egypt. After this incident, he became commonly known as Dhul Nun (The Fish Man).

Dhul Nun Al-Misri was born in Akhmim, a city on the banks of the Nile. His name was Thawban Ibn Ibrahim. He was of Nubian origin and light-skinned. He travelled extensively in Arabia and Syria, seeking knowledge and wisdom. From an early age, Dhul Nun became interested in the arts of mysticism. He went one day to visit a pious man on a mountain. He found him suspended from a tree. The pious man then said aloud to himself: *"O body, assist me in obeying God, or else I will keep you hanging like this until you die of hunger."* Dhul Nun began to weep. *"Who is this, who shows compassion to one whose shame is little and whose sins are many?"* enquired the pious man. Dhul Nun asked him why he tortured himself. The pious man replied: *"This body of mine does not obey God and prefers to keep the company of people. If one socialises with people, then other sins follow."* *"What a great Sufi you are!"* remarked Dhul Nun. The man scoffed at this notion. He informed Dhul Nun that further up the mountain was a far greater ascetic than him.

Dhul Nun proceeded up the mountain, and there he found a man whose foot had been amputated and flung out of his cell. He enquired of the man of what had transpired. The ascetic replied: *"One day, I was sitting in this cell and a woman passed by, and I desired her. I stepped out of the cell. Then I heard a voice say: 'Are you not ashamed that after obeying God for thirty years, you now obey the devil and* chase a woman?' So, I cut off the foot that was already outside the cell. What has brought you to a sinner like me? If you desire to see a man of God, proceed further to the top of this mountain." However, Dhul Nun could not climb the mountain any further. So instead, he asked the ascetic to tell him about this truly pious person. The ascetic replied: "He has been at the top of the mountain for a long time. Once, a man disputed with him, accusing him of being lazy and suggested he try working for his living. The holy man then vowed to place his complete trust in God. He starved himself for a while, and then God sent a cloud of bees to hover around him and provide him honey."

Dhul Nun felt ashamed that he did not possess such trust in God himself. He realised that whoever places his trust in God will be provided for. He had always desired to stay on the path of total reliance upon God, but he had so far been too afraid. As he pondered this matter, a blind bird fluttered down to the barren ground beside him. "Where will this helpless creature get food and water?" Dhul Nun thought to himself. The bird dug at the earth with its beak. Suddenly, two saucers appeared before it – gold, containing grain, and silver, full of rosewater. The bird ate and drank its fill, and then it flew up into the tree, and the saucers vanished. Utterly dumbfounded, Dhul Nun exclaimed: "God is sufficient for us, and He is the best guardian! I repent!" Up to this point, his trust in God was still incomplete. However, after this incident, he completely surrendered. "I will stand at His door until He lets me in," Dhul Nun stated.

In the meantime, he continued his travels. As the sun was about to set one day, he signalled to his companions that they should rest for the night in the desert. Having offered their prayers, the companions began searching for firewood to help prepare the evening meal. Suddenly, there arose a cry of joy: "We are rich! Look at all these jewels!" They all gathered and saw unveiled a huge jar full of gold and jewels. On top of the jar was a tablet bearing the name of God. His companions began to divide up the gold and jewels. However, Dhul Nun shouted: "Take my share too! Just give me the tablet on which the name of my Lord *is written.*" They gave him the tablet, and he accepted it with great reverence, kissed it and held it close to his chest throughout the night. Later in his dream, he heard a voice: "*They preferred the gold and jewels. However, you chose something better, My Name. Therefore, I have opened the door of knowledge and wisdom for you.*" Later, Dhul Nun would return to the city.

One day whilst he was performing his ablutions. His eyes glanced out the window and fell on the roof of the pavilion nearby. On the balcony there, he saw a beautiful girl. As she spoke, he heard her voice clearly: "*Dhul Nun, when you appeared from afar, I thought you were a madman. When you came nearer, I thought maybe you were a scholar. When you came even closer, I was certain you were a mystic. Now I see you are not a madman, nor a scholar, nor a mystic.*" "Why do you say that?" he asked. "*If you had been a madman,*" she replied, "*You would not have made your ablutions. If you had been a scholar, you would not have gazed at that which is prohibited. If you had been a mystic, your eye would never have strayed from God.*" Saying this, she vanished into thin air. Dhul Nun realised that she was not human and had been sent by God to warn him.

Afterwards, Dhul Nun pledged himself to the path of voluntary deprivation. He openly advocated renouncing the lower world in favour of the Hereafter. He chose the 'path of blame' (*malamah*), wherein the people would blame him for his outward conduct while he blamed himself for his inward state. No man can ever attain a great rank unless he regards his actions as a type of hypocrisy and righteousness itself as a presumptuous pretence. If he does this, he is safe from delusion and the chance of falling prey to the ego's trickery.

Adam, the father of humankind, was the exemplar in this tradition of accepting blame. He was famously deceived by the devil, who tempted him and his wife to eat the fatal fruit. Consequently, God banished them from paradise. Adam, admirably, did not resort to blaming anyone besides himself: "*O, Lord! We have sinned against ourselves, and unless You grant us forgiveness and bestow Your mercy upon us, we shall most certainly be lost.*" (7:23). In contrast, the devil himself blamed his downfall on absolutely everyone apart from himself. In the spiritual realm, a saint once asked Adam why he had been blamed for an action that was not in itself a sin. Adam replied: *"If I did not take the blame, then the charge would have gone against God. By taking responsibility, no one could blame my Lord."* There are many such examples of prophets taking the blame upon themselves. Yunus, trapped in the whale's belly, would make the following supplication, even though he was entirely free from sin: *"There is no deity except You; exalted are You. Indeed, I have been of the wrongdoers."* (21:87). The last Messenger, the Prophet ﷺ, continued to observe this tradition. When the Quraysh had enforced a boycott against the Muslims, resulting in children starving and the harsh conditions taking their toll on the old and weak, the Prophet ﷺ made a journey to Taif in the hope of forming an alliance that could offer a haven for the Muslims. The leaders of Taif rejected his call to Islam, and furthermore, they told the boys of the town to pelt the Prophet ﷺ with stones so that blood flowed from his body. The Prophet ﷺ did not curse them and instead prayed: *"O God, maybe it is my fault that I did not invite them properly. Do not punish them; maybe their children or grandchildren will accept Islam."*

Hamdun Al-Qassar (d.884) was once asked: *"What is the path of blame?"* He replied: *"It is to abandon the desire to look good in front of people; to renounce the need to please them; to be at all times beyond blame in fulfilling one's duties to God."* Like much in Sufism, this practice can also be traced back to Ali. One day he heard the Prophet ﷺ announce: *"You are not a true believer until seventy people call you insane."* He immediately set out to fulfil this mandate by behaving bizarrely in public. The people were shocked by his behaviour and his antics. *"What is wrong with Ali? Has he gone mad?"* said one. *"Ali has gone crazy!"* said another. Undaunted, Ali continued in this manner until seventy people had called him deranged.

At least outwardly, the people of 'the way of blame' have no special marks to distinguish them from others. However, Dhul Nun spent his life travelling and meeting such saintly people. He met some disguised as beggars in tattered clothing and others dressed as ordinary folk. He lived inconspicuously amongst the masses for years without ever disclosing their existence.

Meanwhile, Sultan Al-Arifin (804–874) had himself been travelling for many years. Finally, he returned home in the month of Ramadan. He was eager to see his mother, but when he arrived on the outskirts of his town, the people had fully lined the streets to greet him. He thought to himself: *'I will be here for hours if I meet all these people. My poor mother will be left waiting!'* He then pulled a piece of bread from his pocket and ate it in clear view of the crowd. The people were shocked: *"How can a shaykh be so neglectful of the Shariah? If he were truly a man of God, he would observe the fast!"* Disapproving of his actions, one by one, the people dispersed. With the path clear, Sultan Al-Arifin rushed through to see his patient mother. The Shariah, of course, stipulates that it is permissible for a traveller to abstain from fasting. Sultan Al-Arifin was well versed in the Shariah, and he broke his fast to gain the greater reward, the pleasure of his mother.

One master was asked to explain his view on this matter of self-blame. He replied: *"It is inconspicuousness in all matters that should distinguish one in the eyes of people, by one's manner of dressing, walking, or sitting. One should rather adopt the external behaviour of the people in whose company one is. While at the same time, one should be isolated from them by way of contemplation, so that one's outward appearance conforms to society while one's internal reality remains distinguished."*

One of the masters was asked: *"What are the first steps in this affair?"* He answered: *"To humiliate the ego and deprive it of what it relies upon, that with which it finds comfort. Its habit should be inclined towards others, justify the wrongdoings of others, and rebuke one's own self".*

The masters have emphasised the need for constant scrutiny: to watch your every step of the ego's trickery. Praise – be it self-induced or external – is always for some achievement that no longer exists in the present tense. Be it a generous act, a well-performed deed, or a vigil one has kept. So it is truly futile to give it any consideration because a true Sufi lives in the moment, not in the past or the future. Only through practising malamah can one truly achieve genuine sincerity in his actions and deeds. If people's personal views are given priority, then all deeds performed subsequently will carry a foul stench. The Prophet ﷺ reports: *"God says any man who does an action and does it to please other than Me, then I shall have nothing to do with him."*

In fact, to perform actions in such a manner constitutes a kind of 'hidden' shirk (polytheism, idolatry). The Prophet ﷺ warned mankind against this because God will only accept pure actions done for His sake. The Prophet ﷺ mentions: *"On the Day of Judgement, God will say to a group of people, 'Take them to heaven.' They will approach heaven but will not be given access, yet they will be able to smell its beautiful fragrance and see a glimpse of its wondrous beauty. God will bring them before Him, and they will ask: 'O God, if you did not want to give us paradise, why did you show it to us?' And God will say: 'You put everyone in life before Me, and you did everything to please them before Me. Now your place is hellfire.'"*

Dhul Nun once gave this very lesson of true value to one of his disciples. He entrusted him with a diamond, saying: *"Go to the grocery, and buy something, and pay him with this diamond."* The disciple did as instructed. When he gave the diamond, the shopkeeper said: *"What is this? I want the money!"* The disciple returned the goods and came back to his shaykh with the diamond. He told Dhul Nun of what had transpired, and Dhul Nun's reply was: *"It doesn't matter. Take it to the jeweller and ask him, if he wants it."* Upon seeing the diamond, the jeweller offered him his whole shop in exchange. The disciple had not been given permission to sell the diamond, so he returned to tell the shaykh what he had been offered. Dhul Nun explained to him: *"This is the thing: those who know the value will give up everything, but for those who do not know will not even give up a carrot!"*

The 'path of blame' requires that you value the spiritual relationship with Him more than any worldly one. The devotee must be willing to be despised by people to be loved by God. 'They strive in the cause of God and do not fear the blame of a critic.' (5:54) An Ottoman sultan once disguised himself as a commoner and patrolled the shadowy streets of his city. At one point, he came across a corpse of a man that had not been touched for days. The locals informed him that this person was a terrible person who had spent his entire life in shameful activities. *"Was he a Muslim?"* asked the Sultan. The people answered in the affirmative.

"As he was a Muslim," said the Sultan, *"We are duty-bound to at least inform his family and perform his funeral."* The Sultan arranged for the body to be taken to his house. Upon seeing her husband, the wife began weeping. *"May God have mercy on you,"* she prayed, *"You spent all your life hiding. Now look how people treat you– they left your body to rot. They think you are the biggest sinner on earth, but you were a saintly man."* *"My sister,"* spoke the Sultan, *"Please explain what you mean."* The wife replied: *"My husband was a pious man. Every day he bought a bottle of wine and poured it in the gutter to save his Muslim brothers from sinning. He would hire a prostitute for the night but was never intimate with her, just to save his Muslim brothers from sinning. I warned him that people would form a bad opinion of him. He replied, 'It is not for people's sake, it is for God's pleasure'. Each time I'd warn him, he'd playfully say: 'Do not worry, my dear wife. The Sultan will perform my funeral.'"* The Sultan began to weep and said: *"I am the Sultan, and I will arrange for him a state funeral and order the scholars and saints to attend it."*

Shaykh Sulami (937–1021) regards the practitioners of self-blame as being among the highest rank of saints. The practice requires nothing but commitment and hardship. It is only people like Dhul Nun who have dared to undertake this lifestyle. For thirty years, he called men to repent, but only one person ever came to the court of God in full obedience. One day, a prince, travelling with his entourage, passed by the door of the mosque. Dhul Nun saw him and announced: *"No one is more foolish than the weakling who opposes the strong."* *"What words* are these?" enquired the prince. *"Man is a weakling, yet he opposes God, who is strong,"* responded Dhul Nun. The prince grew pale and quickly disappeared. However, the next day, he returned. *"What is the way to Him?"* he asked Dhul Nun. *"There is a lesser way, and there is a greater way,"* Dhul Nun answered. *"Which of the two do you want? If you desire the lesser way, then abandon the world, fleshly desires and give up sinning. However, if you want the greater way, abandon everything but God, and empty your heart of all things."* *"By God, I will choose only the greater way,"* said the prince. The next day he donned a woollen robe, entered the mystic way, and in due course became a saint.

For the people who follow this way, worldly possessions have no value. For the ordinary man, value is placed on relationships, wealth and connections, knowing that these assets will one day become his insurance. However, extraordinary people only place value on their relationship with their Lord, knowing full well that He will immediately come to their aid in their moments of need. Therefore, they are effectively deaf, dumb, and blind to people and the world. A boy once approached Dhul Nun and told him: *"I have a hundred thousand dinars. I want to spend them in your service. I wish to use that gold to help your devotees."* *"Have you reached puberty yet?"* Dhul Nun asked him. *"No,"* he replied. *"Then you are not entitled to spend. Wait with patience until you are of age. And then, if you still wish to spend, return to me,"* said Dhul Nun.

When the boy came of age, he returned and gave all that wealth to the devotees. Sometime later, an emergency arose. No wealth was available to serve the devotees, for they had spent all the money. *"What a pity I do not have another hundred thousand so that I could spend it on these fine men!"* said that same young man. When Dhul Nun heard him speak these words, he knew this young disciple still saw the importance of worldly things and foolishly thought money could solve all problems. He summoned this disciple and instructed him: *"Go to the pharmacist and tell him to give you three dirhams' worth of a particular medicine."* The disciple went to the specialist and later returned with the medicine. *"Put* it in the mortar and crush it," Dhul Nun ordered. *"Then pour on top of it a little oil until it becomes a paste. Make three pellets of it, and pierce each with a needle. Then bring them to me."* The disciple carried out these instructions and returned with the pellets. Dhul Nun rubbed them in his hands and breathed on them, and they became rubies. He then said to the disciple: *"Now take these to the market and have them valued, but do not sell them."* The disciple took the rubies to the market and found they were valued at a thousand dinars each. He returned and told this to Dhul Nun. *"Now put them in the mortar and pound them, and then throw them into the water,"* instructed Dhul Nun. The disciple did as instructed. *"My child,"* said Dhul Nun, *"These devotees are not hungry for lack of bread. If they wanted, they could have all the riches in the world. Instead, they have chosen this path of poverty."* The youth repented. The physical world no longer had any true value in his sight.

Dhul Nun put himself through many gruelling practices and deprived his ego of any of the satisfaction it craved. Once, on the night of Eid, his ego spoke to him directly: *'Dhul Nun, you have starved me all year, but it is the day of Eid tomorrow— treat me to something!'* Dhul Nun replied: *'If you assist me tonight in worship, I will treat you. Do you accept?'* The ego quickly accepted. Dhul Nun remarked: *'Excellent. Then let us stand in worship this night and complete the recitation of the whole Qur'an in two cycles.'* On the day of Eid, the food was placed before him at his table, but he only took a morsel. His devotees implored him to eat more. Dhul Nun explained: *"I took that morsel to fulfil the promise I made with my ego."* Later that day, a man came and presented a dish to Dhul Nun. As he did so, he mentioned that he had desired this dish for some time, and fortunately his wife had prepared it for him that morning. However, the man had just seen the Prophet ﷺ in a dream the previous night. And the Prophet ﷺ had asked of him: *"Do you wish to see me on the Day of Judgement?"* The man raced to reply: *"Of course, O, Prophet of God ﷺ, I would love to see you."* *"Then take this celebratory dish that your wife has made with such great care and offer it to Dhul Nun and give him my greetings. Tell him that it is a command from us,"* instructed the Prophet

ﷺ . Dhul Nun replied: "We are, in truth, the Prophet's ﷺ weakest servants. If it is an order from him, then I shall have to eat."

Yusuf Ibn Husayn, an extremely handsome young man, once travelled from Iran searching for a master. One day, he caught the attention of a princess. She came up to him and offered herself to him. Immediately, he ran and hid so that she could not find him. When he fell asleep in his hiding place, he dreamt of a group of people dressed in green robes, along with one very handsome person seated on a throne. He enquired of the green-robed men about this person. They replied: *"We are Angels, and that person on the throne is prophet Yusuf."* Yusuf Ibn Husayn was suddenly overwhelmed, and he began to cry. *'What have I done to deserve this great honour?'* he thought to himself. Prophet Yusuf descended from the throne and embraced him: *"My son, God is pleased with you for refusing that woman. He has sent me now to give you glad tidings. Every period there is one wondrous man, and the marvel of this age is Dhul Nun Al-Misri. You must find him and remain forever in his company."* Yusuf immediately sought out Dhul Nun and became a devoted disciple.

Dhul Nun lived well into his late eighties before the signs of his death began to appear. He became severely ill and would fall briefly unconscious at regular intervals. His loyal devotee, Yusuf Ibn Husayn, sought his counsel in his last days: *"Master, please give me some advice?"* Dhul Nun replied to him: *"Be with those people who are safe on the outside and the inside. They should remind you of Him and take you to Him."*

Many had cursed Dhul Nun during his lifetime, deeming him crazy and a madman. Some of his enemies went so far as to report him for heresy to the Caliph in Baghdad. On the night of his departure from this world, seventy people in his circle saw the Prophet ﷺ in their dreams. All reported that he explained to them: *"We have come to visit and pay respect to the friend of God, Dhul Nun Al-Misri."* Upon his death, people noticed that there was some green writing on Dhul Nun's forehead. It read: *"This is the friend of God. He died in the love of God.*

He was slain by the sword of God." On the day of his funeral, it was extremely hot. Thousands of birds appeared and hovered together over the procession when they lifted his coffin to carry him to his grave. By flapping their wings, they shaded the bier from Dhul Nun's house to the graveside. As he was being taken along the road, a muezzin chanted the call to prayer. As the muezzin read the shahada (testimony of faith), Dhul Nun was seen to raise his index finger. *"He is alive!"* the people shouted. They laid down the bier. His finger may have been pointing upwards, but he was dead. They tried but could not straighten his finger. When the people of Egypt saw this, they were ashamed and repented.

Dhul Nun had lived a life of hardship and extreme discipline. He cared not for what people thought of him, and his only focus was God. Traversing through the spiritual path, he achieved a great rank. He once said of his life: *"I travelled on three paths. In the first journey, I came across things that I shared with the common people. On the second journey, I came across the type of knowledge only understood by the special ones. On the third journey, I came across knowledge that neither the common people nor the special ones knew."*

"Self-blame is to abandon
the desire to look good
in front of people;
to renounce the need
to please them;
to be at all times beyond
blame in fulfilling
one's duties to God."

Hamdun Al-Qassar

The Most Sacred

TAFSIR

Mawlana Ya'qub Charkhi (1380–1447)

Mawlana Ya'qub is one of our masters in the Naqshbandiyya path. I have read a lot about and by him. He is buried in Tajikistan, and for years I dearly wished to visit him. This wish was fulfilled in 2019. Majid and Saheed compiled the article in 2017.

It has often been said that the Basmala contains the true essence of the Qur'an. It is an expression so magnificent, yet so concise, that all but one chapter of the Qur'an begins with it. The common translation – *'With the name of God, Most Gracious, Most Merciful'* – fails to capture either its true depth of meaning or the inspirational message it signifies. To gain such an understanding is only possible through applying the science of *tafsir* (Qur'anic exegesis). The word *tafsir* is derived from the Arabic word *fasara*, which literally means 'to make something clear.' As the Qur'an was being revealed, whenever a word, sentence or incident was mentioned that the Companions were unclear about, they would ask the Prophet ﷺ to explain it. So, the science of *tafsir* can be said to have begun with the explanations of the Qur'an by the Prophet ﷺ .

Through the blessings of the Prophet ﷺ , this method continued with his Companions and two particularly unique personalities. *"O God, grant him the knowledge of the Qur'an and its interpretation,"* prayed the Prophet ﷺ . Abdullah

Ibn Abbas (619–687) narrated many traditions about the meaning of the Qur'an. He held weekly classes about *tafsir*. Additionally, Abdullah Ibn Masud (594–653) was another person who received his training in the Prophet's ﷺ household. *"Whoever wants to read the Qur'an in as fresh a manner as when it was revealed, let him listen to Abdullah Ibn Masud,"* was the praise given to him by the Prophet ﷺ. Such was the knowledge attained by Abdullah Ibn Masud that he could rattle off where each and every verse of the Qur'an was revealed and the circumstances behind these revelations.

The science of *usul at-tafsir* (principles of *tafsir*) continued to evolve throughout the first three generations of Muslims – the pious predecessors. This scholarship was then undertaken by the major commentators of the Qur'an. This led to a more systematic approach of study amongst all the subsequent generations of Muslims. This form of knowledge is given particular importance in our tradition as it enables Muslims to gain a true and deeper meaning of the Qur'an.

The blessings of the Prophet ﷺ for this science were not limited to those bestowed upon his Companions. The Prophet ﷺ appeared in a dream to Mawlana Ya'qub. He relates: *"I was confused as to which field of knowledge I should study. I had a blessed dream in which the Prophet ﷺ was slowly reciting the Qur'an. As I listened to his beautiful recitation, a thought occurred to me – there must be a reason why he is reciting at this pace. I understood that the Prophet ﷺ was teaching me that the Qur'an should be recited with tajwid (correct pronunciation) and understood with tafsir."* This vision was the indication that Mawlana Ya'qub should devote himself to studying tafsir. Mawlana Ya'qub Ibn Uthman Charkhi was born in the village of Charkh in Ghazni. He belonged to a righteous family. He writes: *"My father was a pious man and followed the Sufi path. He was my first teacher, and he gave some attention to teaching me specific supplications to read after certain Surahs of the Qur'an. One supplication that gave me great joy was to recite Surah An-Naba (The Great News). I followed it up by making the following supplication, 'O God, free our necks, the necks of our parents, the necks of our families and relatives,* the necks of our teachers and the necks of all believers, from the fire of hell. O the Most Merciful of the Merciful.'" He continues: "*Learning from my father led me bearing a great passion in my heart to seek knowledge. Still, I did not have the means to fulfil this burning desire. My situation was resolved when Khidr came to me and said: 'You have my blessings – go and study. Whenever you are in need, all you have to do is call me.' Indeed, this was true, as Khidr did take care of my affairs whenever the need for him arose.*"

"*As a youth, I then travelled to Herat for my education, and there I memorised the Qur'an. I began to study the science of tafsir, as instructed by the Prophet ﷺ. I also studied other sciences, including Islamic jurisprudence, Hadith, and logic. During this time, I also travelled to Egypt, where I was fortunate to benefit from attending the lessons of Al-Shirwani, who had been deemed 'the Encyclopaedia of the Age'. After I completed my studies, I then received official permission to make independent legal decisions. I decided it was now time to return to my country. However, there was still a certain intention remaining that I felt I needed to fulfil. I heard much about a famous spiritual master of Bukhara – Khawaja Bahauddin Naqshband (1318–1389) during my studies, but I had never met him.*"

"*Nonetheless, I had still developed a sincere love for him, and I always intended to visit him one day. I made my way to Bukhara to pay my respects, after which I planned to return home. When I finally met him, I asked him to keep me always in his gaze, hoping for some initiation in the spiritual path. Khawaja Bahauddin Naqshband then replied: 'You came to me on your way back to your country?' I realised that he knew I was a traveller. I mentioned my circumstances and went on to explain the purpose of my visit. I said I wanted to serve him and show him that I was loyal and bore a sincere love for him. He was the master with the greatest fame in the entire region; everyone accepted and admired him. 'That is not a good enough reason for me to accept you,' he remarked. I pleaded with him: 'O my master, the Prophet ﷺ mentions 'If God loves someone, then He will influence the hearts of people to love that person as well.'" Hearing this, he smiled and responded: 'I am the* spiritual inheritor of Azizan. What you say is true.' His mention of the name Azizan surprised me because in a dream I had seen a month earlier, I heard a voice saying to me: 'Be the disciple of Azizan.' I had no idea who he was at the time, but Khawaja Bahauddin Naqshband dropped the name into our conversation as if he had been aware of my dream. I paid him my respects and then asked for his permission to leave."

"I realised that my spiritual link was inevitable with Khawaja Bahauddin. His grandmaster was named Khawaja Azizan (1194–1315). I visited him again, and this time I pleaded for initiation and spiritual focus. Khawaja Bahauddin said: 'Whenever someone asked our blessed Khawaja Azizan for special focus, he would say, 'Leave something from your belongings that will remind me of you – that way, I can focus on you again and again.'' I remained silent and listened; as a student, I felt I had nothing to offer. I also felt Khawaja Bahauddin must already be aware of my circumstances. He then said to me: 'You have nothing to offer, but let me give you a gift by which you will undoubtedly remember me.' He gave me his turban and said: 'When you see this or use it, you will remember me, and whenever you remember me, you will find me – and when you find me, you will find your way to God.' Listening to these words stirred my heart at that moment. I gave him my greetings after gaining permission to leave. Khawaja Bahauddin then said: 'On your way back to your country, if you meet Mawlana Tajuddin – do not gossip even in your heart in his presence. He is a great saint, and he will scold you if you do.' I said to myself, 'I do not think I will see Mawlana Tajuddin, as I am going back to Herat via Balkh. I will not be going through the area where Mawlana Tajuddin lives.' However, the caravan in which I made my return journey had to change its route. So we were forced to travel past Mawlana Tajuddin's area. I remembered the words of Khawaja Bahauddin clearly. It came to my heart that he must have caused events to occur so that I would visit Mawlana Tajuddin."

"When the caravan finally arrived in the area, it was nightfall. I made my way to the mosque to enquire about Mawlana Tajuddin. Inside the mosque, a person approached me and said: 'Are you Ya'qub Charkhi?' The astonishment must have been etched on my face, and so this person said: 'Do not be so surprised. I knew you would be coming here. My master, Khawaja Bahauddin, sent me to take you to Mawlana Tajuddin.' On the way, we met an old man who confided to me: 'O my son, our way is full of surprises. Whoever enters it cannot understand it. The seeker must leave his mind behind.' We then entered the presence of Mawlana Tajuddin. At that moment, it was exceedingly difficult to keep my heart free from any gossip. Mawlana Tajuddin gave me a piece of his spiritual wisdom that I had never heard expressed before. I realised that all I had learned before this meeting was nothing compared to the knowledge he offered me. I was thrilled that Khawaja Bahauddin had arranged for me to meet Mawlana Tajuddin in this way. Sitting in Mawlana Tajuddin's presence, I began to understand why Khawaja Bahauddin had not given me initiation. Mawlana Tajuddin talked about Khawaja Bahauddin continuously. It was self-evident how much love he bore for him. I realised that I had been sent here to comprehend what it meant to love a spiritual master. I decided against continuing my journey home and immediately returned to Bukhara."

"In Bukhara at that time, there lived an intoxicated mystic whom many people visited for blessings. I decided to visit him myself. As he saw me, he told me: 'Quickly go to your objective. What you have decided is best.' He began to draw a series of lines in the dust, and it came to my heart to count these lines. If the number was odd, then it would indicate a good sign for me because the Prophet ﷺ says: 'God is One, and He likes the odd number.' I counted the lines, and they proved to be odd. When I was given permission, I then met Khawaja Bahauddin, and he spoke to me as if he had been with me when I met the mystic: 'Always keep to the odd numbers. Just as you wished the number of lines would be odd, and it gave you a sign to that effect, so keep that same awareness when you make dhikr (remembrance).'"

"My desire for initiation increased ever further. I visited Khawaja Bahauddin frequently, and my love for him grew. One day, I opened the Qur'an to the verse – 'Those are the ones who have been guided by God, so follow their guidance' (6:90).

I was so happy to read that verse that I immediately decided to visit Khawaja Bahauddin. When I arrived, it was as if he had been waiting for me. He said: 'The time of the prayers has come.' After we had completed praying, he added: 'Knowledge is of two kinds. The knowledge of the tongue is external – it is all that is visible. It is audible teaching – the proof of God to His creation. Knowledge of the heart is beneficial knowledge, and it is the knowledge of the prophets. I wish that God grants you the internal knowledge and the knowledge of the heart.'"

"Khawaja Bahauddin went on to mention the Hadith: 'If you sit with the people of Truth, sit with them with a true heart, as they are the spies of the heart.' He continued: 'They can enter and see what is inside your heart. I have been ordered by God, the Prophet ﷺ, and my shaykh not to accept anyone in my way unless God, the Prophet ﷺ, and my shaykh all accept them. So I will find out tonight if you are accepted.' As you might expect, this was the most difficult night of my life, as I feared that I would not be accepted. I prayed Fajr prayers behind Khawaja Bahauddin. When he examined my heart, all my fears disappeared. He said: 'May God bless you. He accepts you, and I accept you. The Prophet ﷺ accepts you, and I accept you.' He then continued to recite the names of each of the masters in the spiritual chain. After completing this, he congratulated me on being accepted and gave me initiation."

"He gave me permission to guide people and told me: 'This spiritual path will be the greatest happiness for you. What we have granted you, you must distribute it among the people. Speak to people and write to them; guide them and instruct them. We have handed you over to God. Stay in touch with Khawaja Alauddin Attar (1340– 1402) and follow his instructions.' I heeded the words of my master and returned to serve Khawaja Alauddin Attar, who then granted me his permission and selected me as his deputy. I returned to my homeland knowing that I had already fulfilled half of the instruction given to me by Khawaja Bahauddin through my service to Khawaja Alauddin Attar. It was now the time to follow the other half of my master's instructions."

Mawlana Ya'qub always remained aware that his master had instructed him to guide and serve people. After returning home, he not only guided people but also devoted his attention to writing books. During this period of his life, he compiled the *Tafsir Ya'qub Charkhi* and numerous other works. When assessing the topics covered in his works, it is clearly noticeable that alongside the subject of *tafsir*, Mawlana Ya'qub paid great attention to the works of the saints (*awliya*). He always emphasised that a person could achieve numerous benefits at a mere glance from their master in his teachings. However, achieving such a glance was still very challenging, and it had to be sincerely earned. Mawlana Ya'qub mentions the importance of love towards the *awliya* in his commentary on the shortest *Surah* in the *Qur'an*, *Surah Kawthar* (Abundance). He explains that when the Prophet ﷺ provided a commentary of this *Surah*, he conjured the enticing image of *Kawthar*– a stream in paradise containing sweet water. However, there is a final condition that people must fulfil before drinking from it: they must show a genuine love towards the Companions of the Prophet ﷺ. Mawlana Ya'qub mentions that fulfilling this condition thus specifically requires people to also show love towards the *awliya*.

The Prophet ﷺ had instructed Mawlana Ya'qub to study *tafsir* and benefit from the commentary of Qadi Al-Baydawi (d.1319). The following examples are some of the profound explanations collected in the *tafsir* of Mawlana Ya'qub:

Bismillah ir-Rahman ir-Rahim: The blessings of this phrase are discussed in-depth. Many narrations similarly mention its importance. Mawlana Ya'qub explains that when a teacher asks a student to recite this phrase, the student utters it perfectly; God rewards the student, the teacher, and the students' parents by freeing all of them from hell's fire. He also notes that God has three thousand names. The blessings of all three thousand names are contained in reciting the word bismillah alone. Mawlana Ya'qub says this is because the *awliya* guide people to say this phrase – they know it has a special blessing. It is viewed as the first gate of guidance, and they want people to achieve this blessing.

Surah Fatiha (The Opening): This *Surah* is known as *Umm Al-Qur'an* as *Umm* (mother) means the source – indeed, it is the first passage of the *Qur'an* itself. Reciting this *Surah* grants the reader the same blessings as if they had just read the entire *Qur'an*. Mawlana Ya'qub adds that some *Qur'anic* commentators spent their entire lives explaining the *Surah Fatiha*. Ali says: *"What is contained in the Qur'an is contained in Surah Fatiha."*

Surah Lahab (The Palm Fibre): In this Surah, Abu Lahab is cursed by God with the words: *"May the hands of Abu Lahab be destroyed."* This was in response to Abu Lahab cursing the Prophet ﷺ , and so, naturally, he suffered an inexorable fate. Mawlana Ya'qub places great emphasis on this *Surah*. It functions as a warning to all people not to oppose the *awliya*. He says, instead: *"Be like Abu Bakr, not Abu Lahab."* He explains that Abu Lahab was a blood relative, but he opposed him and was punished despite this. As such, Mawlana Ya'qub emphasises its importance to remain loyal to the *awliya,* as they are God's chosen friends. To achieve this, people should follow the path of Abu Bakr – a man who was forever sincere and loyal towards the Prophet ﷺ .

Surah at-Tin (The Fig): There are many narrations on record from the Companions about how beautifully the Prophet ﷺ recited this *Surah*. God takes an oath by the fig and olives, which are then consumed by the Prophet ﷺ . God also takes an oath by the city of *Makkah* – the sacred city in which the Prophet ﷺ was born. Mawlana Ya'qub explains that God is, ultimately, taking an oath on His Beloved Prophet ﷺ . He reminds all his readers that He holds complete authority in this world and the Hereafter.

Surah Muzammil (The One wrapped in Garments): God addresses the Prophet ﷺ beautifully in the opening of this *Surah*. Mawlana Ya'qub states that the Prophet ﷺ once touched a piece of bread, and when the piece was placed in a furnace, it failed to burn. Following this symbolic example, he further emphasises the need to show love and loyalty to the Prophet ﷺ. He is the salvation for people. This *Surah* is listed by Mawlana Ya'qub as an essential part of the syllabus for a true believer or anyone who seeks to attain the closeness of God. He categorises it as focusing on three devotional acts: to pray at night, to read the Qur'an and to have a period of seclusion.

Mawlana Ya'qub further explains that the Prophet ﷺ was utterly committed to the practice of *tahajjud* (night prayer). This devotion directly reflects how close a person is to God. Thus, for a believer to attain blessings, worship at night is necessary. The nighttime offers the believer a period to cut themselves off from all worldly activities, remember God, and accrue spiritual benefits. Mawlana Ya'qub narrates in this regard: *"Shaykh Junayd Al-Baghdadi (830–910) once appeared in a dream to a person who asked about his situation in the Hereafter. He mentioned that the most beneficial act of worship was the night prayer."* Mawlana Ya'qub advises that it is only through the recitation of the *Qur'an* that a believer can achieve a greater rank and attain nearness to God. To read and be sincerely connected to the *Qur'an* is a true reflection of a believer's faith. This last *Surah* is thus regarded as being immensely powerful. It removes many difficulties in this life and is a source of blessings for the Hereafter.

There are many possible methods of self-seclusion, but the objective in all is the same: to reconnect the heart with God and focus the mind on worship. Khawaja Bahauddin often stated: *"May God grant us such a passion and desire for Him that we become people of grace. May God accept us and keep us in His grace."* Mawlana Ya'qub dedicated his life to following and implementing the teachings of his master, Khawaja Bahauddin. He passed away in 1447. His shrine is located near Dushanbe, the capital of present-day Tajikistan. Regular visits to Sufi shrines are part of the national religious identity in Tajikistan. The shrine of Mawlana Ya'qub is regarded, unsurprisingly, as one of the most popular in the country. The following account is from one recent visit:

"The complex of Mawlana Ya'qub is situated on the periphery of Dushanbe in a

predominantly impoverished area. The complex has large gates. As you enter, the madrasa can be seen situated to the left, splayed out in endless rows of small rooms, of which only a few are currently in use. The imam uses one, a second is a guestroom to serve food or tea, and it is common to find the local people socialising in a third. There is an open-plan area in the middle, where many plants blossom up alongside vast trees. There is also a noticeable minaret in the courtyard, done in brick fashion with turquoise tiles (most likely a recent addition to the complex). According to the local people, Jami (1414–1492) left his staff behind after his forty-day seclusion. A tree grew on the spot.

Opposite the shrine is the mosque, bearing up a worn-out and rusty dome that reveals its age. It was constructed over five centuries ago. The recent large extension using a design from contemporary local architecture is immediately noticeable. The mosque gets busy at prayer times, with over fifty people steadily present in the congregation. But people also visit the site throughout the day. Although communication with the locals was limited due to the language barrier, everyone seemed friendly and hospitable. There was never a sense of boredom.

The shrine itself is walled, with large windows that visitors can look through. There is a square path around the grave, and people will often leave offerings for the resident imam. The atmosphere around the shrine was peaceful, and while the path to the shrine was roofed, the shrine area itself was open to the sky. Although the locals do not sit near the grave, we were welcome to sit on the raised platform near Mawlana Ya'qub's place. While sitting there peacefully, the thought came to my mind to wonder at how space would have seemed during his lifetime, all those centuries ago."

Today, this sacred place hosts visitors from all over the Islamic world who come seeking blessings and offering their own supplications. A prayer often recited by Mawlana Ya'qub gives a message of hope for all believers: "O God, You are known for your Grace. We are weak, sinful people. What do you expect from us, apart from sins? Forgive us. We do not have any provisions for this journey to You, apart from *the fact that You said, 'Do not despair from My Mercy.' O God, do not make us despair from Your Mercy."*

*"The best of you are those
who learn the Qur'an
and teach it."*

The Prophet Muhammad ﷺ

The Inflicter of Death

DEATH

Beshir Osman Beshir

I vaguely recall that I once met the subject of this chapter at a Sufi centre in Manchester in the early 1980s. I remember him as being slim, tall and very humble. Subsequently, we contacted his widow and son in Madinah, they were surprised to hear that we knew him. Amjid and Sajid compiled the original article in 2008.

If one talks of death, it usually gives the listener shivers and dampens their spirit. However, the remembrance of death should heighten the spirit and reduce worldly desires. It is a fact that we seldom prepare for the inevitable, which is why we fear death. However, some individuals live their lives preparing for the end and are joyous when they meet the Angel of Death.

In a far-away land, there existed a kingdom hidden from the rest of the world. The people of this realm upheld a peculiar tradition. For centuries it was their custom to appoint a king for just three years. Once his term ended, he was taken across the shore to 'the island of no return'; bearing nothing but the clothes, he wore on his back. He was left on this island to die alone. Many such kings came and lived in great pomp and pride for their allotted reign. They enjoyed themselves, with little or no concern for their inevitable, fast-approaching end. However, when their terms ran out, they would begin to worry about their fates.

No matter what they tried, they could not escape the obligatory journey across to the dreaded shore. On the day of travel, the guards would ferry the ex-king across to the island while they busied themselves, selecting their new king.

However, it came to be that one serving king acted very strangely. He did not spend much of his reign indulging in entertainment and leisure. Instead, he chose to fulfil his responsibilities as the ruler. Every day he would make an unnecessary trip to the island of no return. During the second year of his rule, the king became restless and began to talk about settling on the island. As his third and final year began, he seemed even more eager to go. This baffled the people, as they had never seen a king who desired his fate. By contrast, the previous kings were uniformly terrified as they approached the end of their terms.

Meanwhile, the king's wait was over, and the day arrived when the guards came to collect him. They expected him to beg and plead for mercy. They were bewildered to find him full of excitement, asking them to rush him to the island without delay. As the guards reached the island, they disembarked and escorted the ex-king to the shore. He bid the guards farewell and walked towards his new grand palace, which he found surrounded by lush green gardens, streams and waterfalls. These scenic gardens boasted beautiful exotic trees, which bore all kinds of fruits. During his reign, you see, the king had prepared this desolate land by planting these trees, channelling streams and building a luxurious palace for his eventual accommodation. This place looked a thousand times better than the house he had left behind in his kingdom. He had gradually transformed this island of death into a paradise. He had known from the start of his reign that his life as a king would only last a few years, and so he spent his time preparing for the life beyond it.

Nothing in life is guaranteed except death. Life should be lived in its moment and not wasted by dwelling on the past or turning solely to the future. Ibn Umar advises, *'From life take something for the hereafter and prepare for sickness in good health.'* While we still have the opportunity to do so, we should be mindful of death and make the changes in our lives to prepare for it. The Prophet ﷺ says that for a believer, death is a gift. If a person has lived a pious life, God will reward him with the gift of death. He will release him from this abode of deception and introduce him to eternal bliss. Just as a prisoner is rightfully overjoyed when released from captivity, the soul will thank God when freed from the body's constraints.

Only the lovers of the world hate the idea of dying and try everything possible to live that little bit longer. They feel they will always have many unfulfilled desires and wishes. They do not recognise that death is really a bridge to the next world. It is, after all, why we are advised to visit the deceased. At the grave, we tend to contemplate how many wishes the occupant of the grave may have left behind at the time of his death. In such places, we must come to understand that we, too, will inexorably find ourselves in the same situation, just as we will all eventually taste the pangs of death.

Aishah once asked if anyone would stand alongside the martyrs on the Day of Judgement. The Prophet ﷺ replied: *"This honour will be granted to the one who remembers death twenty times in the day and night."* One such person who really did remember death every day of his life was Shaykh Beshir Osman Beshir. Shortly before our time, he was born in Eritrea, and he later settled in Madinah, Saudi Arabia. In this great city, he regularly attended the gatherings of *dhikr* (remembrance) and *Mawlid* (commemoration of the birth of the Prophet ﷺ). However, his tendency was to hide his spirituality, and only a few people ever knew about his inner state. He was viewed as a pious person by the community but never as a spiritual leader.

Hajji Mustafa Ali, a close companion of Shaykh Beshir Osman, relates his story: *"I was once staying at our centre with Shaykh Beshir. Towards the end of his stay in London, after we had passed many nights of dhikr and gatherings, I noticed that the shaykh was more tired than usual. The following morning, I came to the* shaykh's room to deliver his breakfast. As per our routine, I knocked on his door just after dawn, but there was no answer on this occasion. I knocked repeatedly, and still, there was no answer. I began to grow overly concerned as he was always up and ready at this time for his breakfast. I hesitated to open the door without his permission. But after some consideration, I slowly opened the door, saying, 'Allah hu Akbar' repeatedly. Still, there was no response. With even greater concern, I took the liberty of entering the shaykh's room. It was dark, and the curtains were still closed. The room was extremely quiet, and I could see the shaykh's bed. The covers had been lifted over his body like a shroud, and there was no movement beneath. I thought maybe he had passed during the night. So I quickly leapt to the bed with my heart in my throat. I slowly lifted the blanket from his face. His eyes were closed, his body was still, and he looked as though he were dead. I pulled the covers off a little more. To my utter surprise, I found his entire body was wrapped in a burial shroud. Around it, coiled like a snake around the trunk of a tree, was a thousand-bead rosary. My thoughts raced. Had he died in the middle of the night, and someone had secretly come and prepared the body? While such thoughts raced through my mind, the shaykh suddenly moved. Then he opened his eyes. He smiled and greeted me: 'As-Salam Alaykum!' He immediately perceived that I was distressed at what I had just seen, so he asked that I leave his room and return in ten minutes, at which time he would explain everything. I returned as instructed after ten minutes, and he sat me down and explained what had transpired. I learnt that Shaykh Beshir would take a shower each night before sleeping as a preparation for death. He would then wrap himself in a shroud (to the best of his abilities) and lie down upon his bed. He would then recite his wird (litany) with a thousand-bead rosary. This rosary would often become wrapped around him while he turned and shifted in his bed. He explained that this practice was his way of remembering death and that if he did end up dying while asleep, those who would come after to wash and prepare him would simply have less work to do."

In one Hadith, the Prophet ﷺ describes a believer's death as an event 'as painless as pulling a hair out of butter.' Yet in another, he compares the moment to 'the *act of pulling a cloth over sharp thorns, tearing it to shreds.'* One of the masters was, understandably, a little confused about the two disparate traditions. So he started searching for a definitive answer. One evening the Prophet ﷺ visited him in a dream and told him to recite *Surah Yusuf.*

This *Surah* can be summarised as such: The wife of the minister of Egypt, Zulaykha, fell in love once with Yusuf, her slave boy. Zulaykha's friends taunted her, saying she had disgraced herself by falling in love with such a low-ranked suitor. The women themselves had never seen Yusuf. So Zulaykha invited them all to a banquet that she catered for with fruit trays and knives. When Yusuf finally appeared before them, the women happened to be cutting the fruit. They were all so immediately overwhelmed by his beauty that they cut into their hands, slicing their fingers open without a flicker of pain.

The shaykh finished this *Surah,* but still, he could not understand how death - an undeniably painful affair - could seem painless to some people. Once again, he was visited by the Prophet ﷺ . This time he confessed: *"O Messenger of God, I did not understand."* The Prophet ﷺ repeated that the answer to his question was buried in Yusuf's story. He should read it again. The shaykh read and re-read the Surah until he finally reached the story where the women cut themselves without any pain. From this, he belatedly gathered that one would not feel pain if one was absorbed in looking towards God and His Beloved – just as the women had focused on Yusuf, their beloved, and had thus felt no discomfort.

God created our bodies to house two forms: the ego and the soul. If we are ruled solely by the ego, we will chase the physical world and become intoxicated with unquenchable desires. No matter how great our accomplishments are, we will always want more and end up like the smallest of all fish attempting to drink the entire ocean. If we die in such a state, clutching at the world with both hands, then we will surely leave it kicking and screaming when our souls are finally ripped out of our bodies. However, if our souls ride above our egos, we become free from desire and begin to look forward to death. Just as a lover eagerly anticipates meeting with his beloved, the soul lives in anguish, craving a return to its homeland so as just to be in His presence. At this appointed time, we will become like the women at the banquet in Yusuf's story.

The Prophet ﷺ says: *"Remember often the breaker of desires."* This means we must remember death. Through this, our desires are calmed, our hearts and mind made clear.

Imam Al-Ghazali (1058–1111) explains that we burden ourselves with endless desires due to our ignorance and the fact that we constantly delude ourselves that we have plenty of time. A young person will say to himself: *'I have plenty of time - I'll change when I'm mature.'* His response will also change when he is mature: *'I'll do it when I get older.'* Unfortunately for him, when he gets older, he becomes preoccupied with sorting out earthly matters for his children and grandchildren, endlessly delaying what really matters. The Prophet ﷺ says to *'Love whatever you choose to, as long as you recognise that you will be separated from it.'* It is due to their desires that a person becomes attached to the world. This misguided kind of love is what stops them from doing anything positive for the Hereafter. Even when death is contemplated, it makes no real impact on a heart too laden with wants, so the person treats it with very little care. The Prophet ﷺ once drew two lines on the ground - the first being a metre long and the second two metres. He explained that the first line signified a human being's life span and the second his desires. From this, we are to understand that no matter how long we may live, our desires and wants will always surpass our potential.

During his sermon, Umar Ibn Abdul Aziz (682–720) said: *"O people, you have not been created for no reason, and you have not been left without any advice. Know that there is a promised day on which your Lord will gather you in two groups: the unfortunate ones and the fortunate ones."* He then advised his listeners to join the fortunate group and seek not the pleasures of the world. Mawlana Rumi, likewise, says that the world is so devious that it tempts you with bait and catches you if you succumb to it. God declares to His creation: *"O the world! Anyone who is My slave, you shall become his slave. Anyone who wants to become your slave will have no peace in this world or the Hereafter."* Hassan Al-Basri (641–728) mentions that even when he decides not to take a soul, the Angel of Death visits each household three times a day. When he finally does take a soul, he simply stands at the gate and says: *"By God, I have not taken his provisions. I have not deprived him of his decree, nor have I cut short his life by bringing his death forward. O people, I will return again and again until not one of you remains."* Hassan Al-Basri then reports: *"I swear by God, if you were to see him and hear him, you would stop crying over the dead and start crying over yourself!"*

The constant remembrance of death will let the seeker turn cold towards the world and allow them to control all desires. Abu Dharr (d.652) narrates: *"The Prophet ﷺ advised us to visit graves and take time from our lives to wash the dead. These two acts were the best reminders in our world of the Hereafter and thus provided an excellent cure for the heart."* Imam Al-Ghazali explains further that *Shariah* advocates the visiting of graves, especially the shrines of holy people, so that a myriad of holy blessings can be obtained. It has also been narrated that anyone who visits the Prophet's ﷺ grave (the greatest shrine of all) with the proper etiquette will surely oblige him to be his intercessor and witness on the Day of Judgement.

In this regard, Sulayman Ibn Sahim narrates: *"I saw The Prophet ﷺ in a dream, and I asked him, 'O Messenger of God, these people come to you and give salam, do you hear them?' He replied that he hears each salam, and he returns each one."*

A person from the family of Al-Jahdari reports: *"Two years after he died, I saw Asim in a dream, and I asked him where he was now. He replied that he was, indeed, in the gardens of paradise with his companions. I then asked him if he still took note whenever his friends and family visited him at his shrine. He answered: 'We know anyone who visits us from the eve of Thursday until the sunrise on Saturday.'"* Ibn Umar (610–693) never passed by a grave without stopping and giving *salam*.

Imam Jafar (702–765) narrates that Fatimah (605–632) would visit the grave of Hamza (568–625) to recite the *Qu'ran* and offer her prayers nearby. Abu Hurayra (603–678) says that if a man passes a grave and gives his *salam* to it, the grave's occupant will recognise him and return the greeting. Even if the occupant does not know them, they will nonetheless still return the greeting.

Death does not mean the end of everything. Allama Iqbal (1877–1938) explains that those who die do not perish because they simply leave us. During his childhood, Shaykh Nazim (1922–2014) visited the grave of Umm Haram, the Prophet's ﷺ aunt. There it became his habit to sit and discuss diverse matters. Shaykh Abu Ali Ruzbari recalls how once: *"We buried a Darwish. As we placed soil over the body, the Darwish opened his eyes and said: 'O Abu Ali, do you know where I am going?' I then took the chance to ask him if there was a life after death, to which he replied: 'Of course, any lover of God is alive – even after death.'"*

One poet writes of how there is such a joy in death that even the life of Khidr cannot put a measure to it. Rumi explains that we are bound in this world to this world, and so, in death, we become free. Before the Prophet's ﷺ passing, only the people surrounding him could see his noble face. However, in death, almost every day, someone in the world gets to see his blessed face.

When explaining the nature of death, Rumi observes that a ripe fruit falls off a tree very gently, whereas a raw fruit must be pulled harshly from its branch. If one has lived a pious life, one will be like a ripe fruit. However, the same person will be like the raw fruit if they have lived a life of mere desires. When a good person is about to die, the angels arrive in beautiful dresses, appearing in the most handsome forms. They place a silk handkerchief under the dying person's nose so that he may breathe in an intoxicating fragrance while the angels take his soul. Once the soul is free, it is transported to the heavens, where the angels proclaim: *"O Lord, as You know better than anyone, your servant has died, and we have brought his soul to you."* God will reply: *"Open the heavens for him and tell the angels to welcome him in."* The Prophet ﷺ says that he who despises to meet God, God will despise meeting him. So, if the person in question is bad, their soul will not even reach the heavens. The angels will attempt to take the soul there, but the stench of the soul's bad deeds will force it in the opposite direction. The angels will then say: *"Keep them there. Do not bring this wretched person up here. Throw them back to the world."*

As you live, so you will die. If a person lives their life in sin, their end will surely be befitting such a life. Men of understanding explain that 'hell' does not necessarily allude to punishment once a person is dead – a person could be in living hell whilst alive by being habitually engaged in a particular sin. For some, this is drugs, and for others, alcohol – to feed these habits, many deny their children food or clothing and some resort to stealing and murder. They will gain no pleasure from their own actions; in fact, they will only increase their pain and suffering, thus creating their personal hell.

Imam Qushayri (986–1074) describes the deaths of the pious ones by giving some examples of the events of their lives. During his lifetime, Dhul Nun Al-Misri was considered mad by his people. However, three hundred of them saw the Prophet ﷺ in a dream on his death, ordering them to attend his funeral.

Shaykh Nizamuddin (1238–1325) was in Delhi when his master died in Pakpattan, causing him to miss the funeral. Upon arriving in Pakpattan, he sat at his master's grave and wept. Then, suddenly, he became overjoyed. The people asked: *"What happened?"* He replied: *"I saw the Prophet ﷺ come with Abu Bakr, Umar, Uthman, Ali and many other Companions to read the funeral of my master. The Prophet ﷺ also said that anybody who enters through this gate shall go to paradise."* Shaykh Nizamuddin later clarified that the Prophet ﷺ was pointing to the grave of his own master when he referred to this *'gate of paradise'*.

Throughout the history of mankind, the Angel of Death has never asked anyone's permission to enter a household when coming to take a life. However, before the Prophet ﷺ passed away, he asked permission for the first and last time.

Close to death, the Prophet ﷺ asked his daughter, Fatimah, to come closer, and as she did, he whispered something into her ear that first made her cry and then made her smile. When the witnesses asked why she did this, Fatimah replied: *"The Prophet ﷺ told me that he will pass away, and that's what made me cry. Then he told me that out of all his family, I would be the first one to meet with him, and so I smiled."*

None will have any control over death. Imam Al-Ghazali remarks that the Prophet's ﷺ life was beautiful, as was his death. During his last moments, the Prophet ﷺ underwent much pain, his colour constantly changing as he perspired. Imam Al-Ghazali advises us to take a lesson from this: we must consider our state at the prescribed time and look within ourselves to determine whether we are closer to the wrongdoers or to God. The Prophet ﷺ suffered during his passing because when the Angel of Death visited him, the Prophet ﷺ asked him how painful it was to die. The Angel explained that it truly was a very painful experience. So the Prophet ﷺ asked for death to be made easy for his nation. He took on the suffering of the nation at his own passing.

In his well-known poem, Abu Madyan Al-Ghawth (1126–1198) notes that you must lose yourself in your brothers and sacrifice yourself for them to accomplish the noblest of deaths.

Shaykh Muhammad Zahid (1448–1529), the deputy of Khwaja Ubaydullah Ahrar (1404–1490), narrates in this regard: *"Once, Khwaja Ubaydullah Ahrar became severely ill. His devotee Qasim came and said to me: 'Quickly, go and get the doctor because I cannot see my shaykh in this state.' I travelled from Samarqand to Herat and returned to the master after thirty-five days. Upon returning, I found that Khwaja Ubaydullah Ahrar was in good health, and it was Qasim who had died. I asked how exactly Qasim had died, as he was not ill. I was told that he had gone to Khwaja Ubaydullah Ahrar and said: 'I give my life to you, O my master.' He was told by our master not to sacrifice his life for him, as he had a family and was still only a young man. Still, he replied: 'I have not come here to argue. I have already given my*

life to you. I am only here to pay my respects, as God has accepted my supplication.'
He died on the following day of the same illness as that of our master."

Many evil people in history have felt that they had no hope of salvation left to them. Yet, some incident would lead such people towards this type of sacrifice. A young shaykh was once travelling with a few of his devotees. There was a collision on the way, and the driver tried to save his shaykh by swerving the car so it would crash on its side. He died, but he saved his shaykh. Later his shaykh commented, "We have heard stories of the olden times in which devotees risked their lives to save their masters. Now we have seen it with our own eyes."

Hajji Mustafa Ali picks up our narration: "I met Shaykh Beshir Osman when he was well into his seventies. The last time I was with him was around 1984. After an extended visit in London, I accompanied him to Victoria Station, where he was on his way to the airport flying home to Madinah.

At the station, there were a few moments before the train left, so I remained there. Before the last whistle blew, he took my entire face in his hands and kissed me affectionately on my lips. He had never done this before. He then placed his hand over my head and prayed over me, reciting verses from the Qur'an as well as combinations of the Attributes (names) of God. As he prayed, I noticed a tear running down his face. I kissed his hand as I had done so many times before upon taking his leave. As I disembarked the train, I began to feel an ominous sinking sensation that began in my chest, spreading to my entire body. As the train left the station, I burst into deep and mournful tears, as though I was at the funeral of a loved one. I wept so intensely that people around me at Victoria station were touched and approached me offering comfort and solace. I could not explain to them what had come over me because I did not entirely know myself. That was the last time I saw Shaykh Beshir Osman in this world. He passed away shortly after our visit into the next life. Before he passed away, he wrote a letter to my teacher and guide, Shaykh Fadhlalla Haeri. In it, he said that he loved me like a son and when a shadow passed across him from behind or to the side, he would think that it *was I bringing some tea or food to share with him."*

Shaykh Beshir Osman is buried in the Al-Baqi graveyard in the holy city of Madinah.

"And spend [in the way of God] from what We have provided you before death approaches one of you and he says, 'My Lord, if only You would delay me for a brief term so I would give charity and be of the righteous.' But God never delays a soul when its appointed time comes. And God is All-Aware of what you do."

The Holy Qu'ran [63:10–11]

The Magnificent

FEAR OF GOD

Hassan Al-Basri (642–728)

I have read stories concerning the life of Imam Hassan Al-Basri since my youth. I have always admired both his vast knowledge and intense piety. Sayyid Amjid and Sajid compiled the original article in 2007.

> *The death of the God-fearing is eternal life.*
> *Some have died but are still among the living.*

Ka'ab Ibn Malik was one of the three Companions who failed to participate in the Tabuk expedition. As these three had no excuse for their absence, the Prophet ﷺ was terribly upset with them, and he showed his displeasure by turning his face away from them. Consequently, even the Sahabah boycotted all three of them. None of the faithful were prepared to associate with them, speak to them, or even respond to their greetings. It seemed as if they were simply non-existent or that the whole earth, vast as it is, no longer had a place for them. They became outcasts in their own city. Ka'ab says that during this time, he lived in a constant state of fear. He was traumatised in knowing that the Prophet ﷺ was displeased with him. He felt that his heart was constantly exploding and that his soul was crying out from fear of what would happen now. He feared his fate, as he did not know what would happen to him for upsetting the Messenger of God ﷺ. He feared God's inevitable punishment, as it seemed to him that he had assented to the greatest sin that could ever have been committed by anyone. However, his greatest worry was that the Prophet ﷺ would not lead the prayer at his funeral if he died in this condition. That outcome would result in complete destruction for him in the Hereafter.

Additionally, if the Prophet ﷺ himself passed away in the meantime, then, again, he would be doomed forever. No one would ever talk to him again, and no one would pray at his funeral. Thus, for this period, he stumbled around like a living corpse, crying and weeping, suffering day and night, and yet he could not even wish for death because he feared to face his Lord. It seemed to him that this sad state of constant fear had already lasted an eternity.

God has blessed His creation with infinite blessings drawn from His endless oceans of mercy. As everything is from Him and will one day return to Him, there is no doubt that we will have to answer for our lives on the Day of Reckoning, when one and all shall stand before the Lord of Creation. So it is best to consider your actions in this life right now and try to recognise their possible consequences. The pious ones constantly remind themselves of this fast-approaching day. They tremble with fear at the thought of having to finally face their Lord. Hassan Al-Basri's life is, in this regard, the epitome of the rightful fear of God.

Hassan was born in Madinah in 642. His father, Yasar, embraced Islam during the caliphate of Abu Bakr (573–634) and was a freed slave of Zayd Ibn Thabit (610–665). Hassan's mother, Khayriyyah, was the maidservant of Umm Salmah (580–680), the Prophet's ﷺ noble wife. As a baby, he was brought to Caliph Umar, who carried out the *tahniq* (sweetening) and told his parents: *"Name him Hassan because he has a beautiful face."* Umar then prayed: *"O God, make him wise in the religion and beloved to the people."* While his mother was busy doing the housework, baby Hassan cried so much that Umm Salmah breastfed him a little while later. It is said that: "Those few drops of milk he drank from Umm Salmah brought him countless blessings."

When Hassan was still young, he committed an act that he considered to be a major sin. He wrote this act down and wore the note around his neck in the form of an amulet. Whenever he remembered this sin, he would faint from sheer fear of God. In later life, Hassan moved to Basrah, in Iraq. He met one hundred and thirty Companions there, including seventy who had fought at the Battle of Badr. Hassan was not only an exceptionally beautiful child but also grew up to become a very handsome young man. On Friday, Basrah's women would go to the market to talk and ask one another whom they deemed the most handsome man in the city.

When they'd all seen him, they unanimously agreed it was Hassan — the man with the black turban. Throughout this time, Hassan constantly remained in the state of ablution. One night, his sleep was disturbed more than seventy times, and each time he awoke, he performed ablution and prayed two units. He would frequently say to his fellow believers: *"Piety is the basis of the religion. Desire and greed destroy this foundation."* Despite this good sense, he always regarded himself as the worst of all people. Once, when someone asked him: *"Hassan, who's better: you or the dog?"* He responded: *"If I am saved from God's punishment, then I am indeed better than the dog. But if I am seized by God's punishment, the dog is a thousand times better than I."* On another occasion, someone asked him: *"Are you satisfied that a lot of people come to your gatherings?"* Hassan replied: *"I am not happy at seeing a large crowd. I would be quite happy if only two sincere people came."* Once, he was asked: *"Where are Muslims? And where is Islam?"* He replied: *"Muslims are buried in their graves, and Islam is only found in books."* Hassan was busy giving a public talk on another occasion when someone shouted to him: *"What you say does not affect us because our hearts are asleep!"* Hassan replied: *"I wish your hearts were asleep because if they were, I could wake them. Your hearts are dead! No matter how much I try and stir them, they do not move."*

Al-A'mash (680–765) comments that: *"Hassan always accumulated wisdom, and then disseminated it to others."* Imam Muhammad Baqir (676–733) says: *"Hassan's speech resembled the speech of the Prophets."* One day, a person walked past Hassan's room and felt a few droplets of water as they fell upon his robe. He immediately asked aloud if the water that fell was clean. The drops were, in fact, the tears of Hassan, who then replied to him: *"Please wash your clothes, as these teardrops are those of a sinful person."* Once, he accompanied a funeral procession to the cemetery, where he stood by the graveside and began to cry. Then he proclaimed: *"People beware! The end of the world and the beginning of the Hereafter is the grave! The Prophet ﷺ said that the grave is the first of the stations of the Hereafter. Why love such a world when this is its end? Why do you not fear the Day of Judgement, knowing what awaits you?"*

Whenever Hassan walked past people, he appeared to them as if he was being led to his execution. One day, he asked a man why he was crying. The man replied: *"I was in the gathering of Muhammad Ibn Kalb. He told me the story of a person who, on the Day of Judgement, will be thrown into hellfire for a thousand years because of his sins and then will be released."* Hassan immediately prayed: *"If only I could be that person – at least his salvation is certain."*

During a famine, thousands of people from Basrah came to read the rain prayer, and they asked Hassan to lead it. He replied: *"If you want it to rain, then you must throw me out of Basrah!"* He believed that it was because of him that the people were being punished.

One of Hassan's followers was Habib Al-Ajami (d.738), who said: *"When Hassan made a supplication, he would spread his cloak and hands. From this, we could all see that the supplication had been accepted."* Once, Hassan talked to his students when he remarked to them: *"You all remind me of the Companions of the Prophet ﷺ ."* The students were overjoyed by this compliment. Hassan clarified: *"I mean, you resemble them physically. Otherwise, you have nothing in common with them. If your eyes fell on them, you would think they were all crazy, as their devotion and fear of God were beyond your belief. However, if they were to see you, they would not consider any of you to be Muslims!"* A stranger in the city had a wild horse he was trying to sell. Eventually, he came across Hassan, whom he convinced to take it off his hands. That night, that person had a dream in which he saw that whoever ended up owning the horse would go to heaven. As soon as he awoke, he immediately raced to search for Hassan, eager to retrieve the horse. Hassan told him: *"That dream you had – I had the same dream before you."* The man left with a heavy heart. During the night, Hassan then had another dream in which he saw a beautiful house in paradise and asked aloud: *"Who is this for?"* He heard: *"This is for the one who will return the horse."* The following morning, Hassan sought out the man and returned the horse. A pious person narrates: *"I went to the mosque one day before dawn. I saw Hassan making his supplication, and I heard many people saying to him, 'may God accept your prayer'. I did not want to disturb him, so I sat to one side and waited. Later I approached him, and I realised that he was alone. I had heard many voices, so I asked him: 'Please tell me, for the sake of God, what is going on?' Hassan replied: 'Do not tell anyone what you have seen today. On Thursday night, the angels come from the heavens to sit and learn from me, and as I was doing the final prayer earlier, they said amen. That is the sound you heard.'"*

During this time, Hassan happened to have a neighbour named Shamum, who was Zoroastrian. Shamum fell ill and was at death's door, so Hassan visited him and found him in bed; his skin blackened with fire and smoke. He announced to him: *"Fear God! You have passed all your life worshipping mere fire and smoke. Accept Islam now, that God may have mercy on you."* Shamum replied: *"Three things hold me back from becoming a Muslim. The first is that Muslims speak ill of the world, yet both night and day, they pursue worldly things. Secondly, they say that death is a reality, yet they make no proper preparation for it. Thirdly, they say that God's Face shall be seen; yet they seemingly do everything to anger Him these days. I fail to see Muslims carrying out His will or doing anything to please Him."* Hassan then replied: *"What you have said is true. Now, if believers act as you describe, then what have you to say? Believers acknowledge God's unity, whereas you have spent your entire life lost to the worship of fire. You have worshipped fire for seventy years while I have worshipped God. If we are both carried off to hell, it will consume both you and me. If so, God will pay no regard to you, but if He wills it, the fire of hell will not dare to burn one hair on my body. Fire is a thing created by God, and creation is subject to the Creator's command. Come, as you have worshipped fire as your deity all your life, let us both put our hands into the fire. You will see with your own eyes the impotence of fire and the omnipotence of the Almighty!"* So saying this, Hassan thrust his hand into the fire and held it there. And indeed, not a single hair was affected or burnt. When Shamum saw this, he lay amazed, and then, through God's grace, the dawn of true knowledge began to break within him. Shamum groaned from pain: *"For seventy years, I have worshipped fire, and now only a breath or two remains to me. What am I to do?"* Hassan replied: *"Recite the shahadah (testimony of faith) and become a Muslim."* Shamum replied: *"If you give it to me in writing that God will not punish me for my past beliefs, then I will believe in Him."* Hassan wrote what Shamum wanted and then had the inscription endorsed by witnesses at his request. Shamum then wept remorsefully whilst reciting the *shahadah* to Hassan. He then instructed him: *"When I die, wash me and commit me to the earth with your own hands. Place this document in my hand, as it will be my proof for the Hereafter."* Having said this, he recited the *shahadah* one last time and gave up his soul. After washing his body, the funeral prayer was read over him, and he was buried in the grave with the document in his hand.

Later that night, Hassan was restless, finding himself unable to sleep. He was concerned that he had guaranteed a Zoroastrian a place in paradise when he felt he had no authority to do so. *"How can I help a drowning man, seeing that I am drowning myself? Since I have no control over my fate, how can I have power over God's kingdom? Why did I venture to prescribe how the Almighty should act?"* He finally fell asleep, still lost in this thought. But as he dreamed, he saw Shamum radiant as the full moon in all its glory. His neighbour now wore a jewelled crown, with a beautiful robe wrapped around his body. Shamum smiled as he walked into the garden of paradise. Hassan asked him: *"How are you, Shamum?"* Shamum replied: *"Why do you ask? You can see where I am! God Almighty, of His bounty, brought me near His presence and graciously showed me His face. The favours He showered upon me surpass all description. You have honoured your guarantee, so take your document. I have no further need of it."* When Hassan woke up, he saw the same parchment in his hand. Shaking with tears of fear and hope, he prayed: *"O my Lord, I know well that everything You do is done with true purpose and encompassed in Your mercy, and that nothing is without Your grace. Who can ever suffer a loss at Your door? You grant a fire worshipper of seventy years to come near Your presence because of one single utterance. How then can You deny the one who has been worshipping You for seventy years?"*

Abu Amr, a scholar and leading authority on the recitation of the *Qur'an,* was busy teaching one day when a handsome boy arrived to join his class. Abu Amr gazed at the child, wondered at his beauty, and developed evil intentions towards him. Despite his scholarship, he immediately forgot the entire *Qur'an.* Such a fire possessed him that he lost all self-control. In this state, he ran to Hassan and begged him to intercede. *"My master,"* he wept bitterly, *"Such is my situation that I have forgotten the whole Qur'an. Please help me gain forgiveness."* Hassan became distressed after listening to Abu Amr, and so he told him: *"Now is the time of pilgrimage, go and perform Hajj. After you have done this, you must go to the mosque of Khayf. There you will see an old man sitting in the mihrab (prayer niche). Only approach him after he has completed his worship, and then ask him to pray for you."*

Abu Amr did as he was told. When he arrived at the mosque of Khayf in Mina, he saw an old man sitting in the corner. This man had such a powerful aura about him that he was not easy to approach. Abu Amr noticed that many people were also seated around him. After a little while, a very handsome man in beautiful white robes approached him and sat beside him. After taking a breath, the handsome visitor got up and then left the mosque with the rest of the company, leaving only the old man and Abu Amr behind. Abu Amr took this opportunity to approach him and pleaded: *"In God's name, please help me!"* He then described the situation that had befallen him. In response, the old man soon became overly concerned for him and raised his eyes to the heavens and prayed. Abu Amr later recounted: "He had not yet even lowered his head when the entire glorious Qur'an came back to me, and I fell at his feet out of joy and gratitude." Then the man asked Abu Amr: *"Who sent you to me?"* Abu Amr replied: *"It was Hassan of Basrah who sent me to you."*

The man in white robes who entered and then left with the rest was Hassan Al-Basri. The shaykh then asked: *"Anyone who has an imam the likes of Hassan surely has no use of me. As Hassan has exposed me to you by lifting my veil, I will now lift his. Every day he prays his Dhuhr prayer in Basrah, then comes here to bless me with his company, and then returns to Basrah for the Asr prayer."*

Umar Ibn Abdul Aziz once wrote a letter to Hassan, which read in part: *"Please advise me briefly so that I can remember your wisdom."* He replied: *"Remember the time of your death. Live your life, remembering that you are going to die and then be questioned."*

Malik Ibn Dinar (d.748) once asked Hassan: *"What is the disease of the heart?"* *"The love for the world,"* Hassan replied. Once, Hassan saw a young man laugh out loud, and so he questioned him and asked: *"Have you already crossed the Bridge?"* The young man, shocked and confused, answered: *"No."* Hassan then asked him: *"Do you know whether you are going to enter paradise or hell?"* The youth replied: *"I do not know."* Hassan asked: *"Why then this laughter?"*

Once, Hassan overheard a man reciting the Hadith: *"A man will eventually be together with the one whom he loves."* Hassan immediately shouted: *"Do not be deceived! This companionship will only be acquired if you practice the same honourable and pious deeds as the person whom you claim to love!"* Whenever anyone spoke ill of Hassan, he would send them dates with the message: *"Your gift of rewards is vastly superior to my insignificant gift of dates!"*

Hassan also said: *"Not praying tahajjud can only occur because of a sin committed."* To pray the tahajjud, a person must reflect on their day each evening before going to bed. They must repent for any sin they committed and praise God for any good deed they may have had the opportunity to perform. Tahajjud is difficult only for a person who carries no fear and is engaged in sin.

Hassan once said: *"When God intends to do good to a servant, He detaches his heart from the bonds of his family and the world."* When a man once complained to Hassan about the hardness of his heart, he advised him: *"Attend gatherings of dhikr."*

Hassan said: *"True repentance brings you closer to God."*

Hassan once related: *"I have met such awliya whose distaste even for halal exceeds your dislike for haram."*

Hassan said: *"I swear by God! He shall disgrace a person who loves money."*

Somebody once asked Hassan: *"If the doctor is ill himself, can he cure others?"* Hassan simply replied: *"First, cure yourself, and then think of curing others."*

Although Hassan always lived in a state of spiritual terror, people were surprised to see him start smiling when he reached his final moments. As soon as he could, he eagerly gave up his soul to his Lord. Once, in a dream, a beloved friend of God asked Hassan why he smiled at the time of his death. He replied: *"At the time of my death, I heard a voice saying: 'O Angel of Death, be harsh with him. There yet remains a sin on him.' I was pleased to hear this, and I joyously asked about the sin."* Hassan passed into the Divine Presence at the great age of 89. On that very night, another pious person had a dream in which he saw the portals of heaven open and heard a voice proclaim: *"Rejoice! Hassan Al-Basri has reached his Lord! Hassan has surpassed us because the whole creation needs his knowledge, while he needs none besides God. He is, therefore, our master."*

"Do not sit idle for death is seeking you."

Hassan Al-Basri

The Responsive One

WIRD (LITANY)

Salih Al-Jafari (1910–1979)

When I visited Cairo in 2011, I was not familiar with Shaykh Salih. I once listened to a beautiful qasida named 'Radeena', about the Ahl Al-Bayt. I later discovered it had been written by Shaykh Salih. After that, his poems became a regular feature of our gatherings. I learned everything I could about his life and poetry. I finally visited him in 2017. Saqib and Afdal wrote the original article in 2014.

> *'They will abandon you if you forsake their litanies,*
> *so, rise to perform your recitations, do not stay away!*

Each pious person in a spiritual order possesses a special power later passed down to their followers. This is known as a wird. This can only be prescribed by a shaykh to his followers. It cannot be self-diagnosed, just as only a doctor can prescribe a certain medicine. Likewise, a shaykh knows exactly which litany to prescribe for his devotees. A litany is something performed through repetition. If it is a consistent form of action, it can probably be classified as a litany. Each wird has its own optimum hour to be carried out, whether in the morning, afternoon, or night. Some must be carried out on a certain day of the week to achieve its most beneficial effect on the devotee. This is also a form of 'transmission' between a master and his disciple, in both physical and spiritual.

One pious individual who emphasised the value of transmission was Shaykh Salih Al-Ja'fari. He regarded the practice of the litany so highly that he once composed a poem proclaiming its importance. He wrote:

> *You left a litany, but had you known its status,*
> *You would have cried for neglecting it!*

Shaykh Salih was a descendant of the Prophet ﷺ. His lineage traces back to the great Imam Ja'far as-Sadiq. Hence, he was given the surname Ja'fari. His family had originally migrated from Hijaz to North Africa, then to Morocco and then eventually into Sudan, where Salih was born in the year 1910 in the town of Dongola. Muhammad, the father of Salih, had desired to name his first-born son after his own father. Muhammad's father was called Salih, who had once informed him: *"If you name him after me, then you will be giving him as a gift to God; his life will be devoted to God. Therefore, he will be of no use to you in cultivating crops and agriculture."* Muhammad accepted this fate anyway, and so he named his son Salih.

Salih's father taught him about farming and agriculture. He continually stressed the importance of the land, though Salih plainly had no interest in farming. This, at times, angered his father. He took this complaint to Salih's teacher, Shaykh Muhammad. Shaykh Muhammad remarked: *"Do you not remember the promise you made to your own father? You had given him as a gift to God. Forget about the duties you've given him; he is of no use to you now."* It turned out Salih had no desire for worldly affairs at all. From a very early age, he kept himself busy solely with religious studies. He was naturally excited to read and study the Qur'an. He kept the Qur'an beside his bed, reciting it without fail. He had an excellent education and learnt from the local teachers and scholars within his area. At the tender age of fourteen, he had finished memorising the Qur'an, and a few years later, he married.

Shaykh Muhammad was Salih's teacher and the third shaykh in the Idrisiyyah

Sufi Order founded by Shaykh Ahmad Ibn Idris (1760–1837). Shaykh Muhammad was fond of Salih and often referred to him casually as *'our master'*. Salih blushed whenever he heard this, as he thought he did not deserve such a title. At nineteen, he decided to commit to being a devotee of his teacher, Shaykh Muhammad. He was given the *wird*, and he began to have mystical experiences. In his dreams, he would see some of the masters of the *Idrisiyyah Order*. Once he saw Shaykh Ahmad Ibn Idris, who told him personally: *"God is with you, so go study the jurisprudence of the four schools of law."* Salih later had this dream interpreted and discovered that he must go to the region's centre of knowledge and learning, known as the *Al–Azhar University*. His teacher often mentioned that Salih had great potential and encouraged his father to send him to Al-Azhar.

Around this time, Salih borrowed Imam Nawawi's commentary on Sahih Muslim. While studying the book, he once saw Shaykh Abdul Ali (son of Ahmad Ibn Idris) in a dream. He was sitting on a chair with his bags packed. Salih heard someone say aloud: *"The shaykh wants to travel to Al-Azhar."* Salih felt this was a spiritual indication and approval of his journey. He took the chance to greet and kiss Shaykh Abdul Ali, who told him: *"Knowledge is taken from men's chests and not from books,"* and then repeated the statement. Salih later narrated: *"I awoke from my sleep and felt inspired to sit in the company of my local scholars."*

One day, Salih was sitting in his teacher's class when it came to his heart that the Prophet ﷺ may be present in the gathering. As this thought entered his heart, the shaykh looked at him and said: *"Yes, he is."*

> *Hold firmly to our path, and you will get what you seek,*
> *Come to us, and we will reach you!*

The Prophet ﷺ instructed certain of his Companions to recite individual chapters of the Qur'an along with supplications, and these were known as *hizbs*. He would recommend to his Companions to recite *Surah Yasin* in the morning, *Surah Waqi'ah* after Maghrib, and the verse of *'The Throne'* whenever they entered or left their homes (as well as just before sleeping). These are just a few examples of litanies that were set by the Prophet ﷺ. In ordinary people, the litanies act as antidotes for bad characteristics and as catalysts for good virtues. According to the disciple's level, the shaykh must give litanies and increase or decrease the prescriptions depending on the circumstances. The saints follow in the Prophet ﷺ footsteps, using the same principles and applying them to their own followers.

Some litanies granted to the devotees are only spoken within a certain spiritual order and are particularly unique. They have been passed down from the masters within a spiritual chain. When you call upon these litanies, you may gain the attention and focus of all the masters within that chain. They can watch your physical and spiritual state as you recite them. They see your intentions clearly, recognise your capacities and have the power to build connections with your living spiritual master, instructing him on what actions he should carry out with regards to your development. Salih mentions that if you abandon your litanies, then, surely, your master will abandon you. The litanies act as a lifeline between you and your master. If they are abandoned, then the focus of your master may be lost, and someone else will come to benefit from your selfish behaviour. The *wird* is an essential element of your progress and functions like water for the soul.

As mentioned, each *wird* has its own character and personality. The *wird* given to you inevitably influences your temperament. Some may have a soothing effect, while others can make you mercurial and even aggressive if they are not practised with care. Therefore, being the master is never a simple role, especially when distributing the *wird* according to the devotees temperaments and occupations. A *wird* will always have a significant effect on the physical being of a follower. Some litanies are even only given to married men, as they have reached a point in their life where they can carry it well and allow it to influence the heart.

The Prophet ﷺ mentions that if a person was to miss out on one *wird*, he could make it up the next day between morning and afternoon prayer. This is the concession given to them, and it emphasises the extreme importance of the practice. If the litany is read within the time allowed, it will be written down as if it had been read the night before. Salih, however, always managed to keep his *wird*.

As mentioned, Salih intended to move to Al-Azhar, one of the world's oldest universities, based in Cairo. Salih was twenty years old and already married with two children: Abdul Ghani and Fatima. He set off from Dongola and made the arduous journey to Al-Azhar with his family in tow. It is said that when the foundations were being laid for Al-Azhar, the local saints of Egypt had a dream in which the Prophet ﷺ indicated the best (and final) site on which to build the university.

Upon his arrival in the city, Salih was shocked at the cosmopolitan culture of Cairo. He first went to pay his respects to the tomb of Imam Husayn. There he met Shaykh Ibrahim Samaluti. Salih immediately sensed this was not an ordinary person. He would later learn that Shaykh Samaluti was one of Al-Azhar's most prominent scholars. Shaykh Samaluti said to him then: *"Do not think the friends of God only live in caves, separate from society. The true friend of God is he who lives among the scorpions, knowing they cannot sting him. Remain here forever and struggle against yourself and with the people."* Hearing these words, Salih thought to himself: *'This is a man of God. I have not said anything, yet he has read my mind.'* Salih made a firm commitment to remain in Cairo and not to leave it while he still lived. Shaykh Samaluti's day job was teaching the science of Hadith, and Salih began to attend his lectures. With each new session, he began to feel a surge of spirituality stemming from his teacher's wisdom. He later commented: *"Whenever the shaykh mentioned a Hadith, it felt as though the Prophet ﷺ was speaking."*

For in this path, some masters have perfected,
The good counselling of men and God has clothed them in majesty.

Along with Shaykh Samaluti, Salih encountered many other noble teachers throughout his Al-Azhar studies. After spending more time on the campus, he realised that these teachers were not ordinary scholars but members of the *awliya*. They always showed the utmost piety and were indeed the most God-fearing people he had ever come across, each possessing an unbreakable connection with God and the Prophet ﷺ. Salih narrates: *"When I came to Al-Azhar, I discovered a shaykh teaching at every pillar. They were so connected to their teachings that tears used to flow from their eyes. Whenever we sat in their presence, we were humbled and would cry at how their words touched us, such was their obvious sincerity and connection with God."* These people were not mere scholars that had memorised books - they possessed and shared much more. Salih narrates: *"One night, I saw the Prophet ﷺ in my sleep, and he referred to me as a boy. I was angered by this, and I thought to myself: 'What have I done wrong?' When I woke up, I went to my lesson, and I sat in dejection at having been called a boy by the Prophet ﷺ. It felt as though I was simply not mature enough for the path I was on. As I was thinking this, the shaykh in the class turned to me and said: 'It is not meant in that context; we only call you boy because it is the custom of the Arabs. It is because you are young.' These people are true saints. They are the people that receive direct knowledge into the hearts in the form of divine inspiration."* Shaykh Habibullah was another of Salih's notable teachers. He had previously taught for many years in Makkah and was a distinguished scholar. He would pick a reciter from his class to read the Qur'an and *Hadith* – a role reserved only for the most intelligent and brightest student. Salih wished to recite in his lessons, and so one day, he went over to his teacher's house and knocked on the door, shaking in anticipation. As he opened the door, he immediately said to Salih: *"God willing, you are the one."* Without Salih uttering a single letter, he had gained his approval and had been given his permission to recite.

Salih, at times, would lead the lesson when his teacher was ill. Hence, this meant that he would end up delivering the class himself to his fellow students. Inevitably, they would often mock him for this and make his life difficult. With this frustration in mind, Salih eventually approached his teacher and informed him of the situation. Shaykh Habibullah sympathised and told him: *"They only mock you because they are jealous of you - do not be disheartened by them."* At times, Shaykh Habibullah would correct him on the lesson he had just delivered. This would be done without Salih telling his teacher what he had even spoken about. This alone indicates the level of Shaykh Habibullah's insight. Shaykh Habibullah often stated: *"Shaykh Salih is the blessing of the lesson, and he has the authority to teach and give permission to anyone, at least from what I have received."* Salih held an immense love and loyalty towards his teacher and later stated: *"I stayed with Shaykh Habibullah until his death, remaining his student for 15 years. I was involved in his burial, and afterwards, I began to teach in the mosque of Imam Husayn."* Shaykh Salih had completed his studies and gained the highest honours possible in 1942. Then he finally travelled back to Sudan to celebrate this achievement with his extended family. He was offered a job at Al-Azhar, and in 1947 he was appointed senior shaykh. He never gave up his studies and continued to strive until he was given a PhD in Islamic sciences.

Shaykh Muhammad once came to Cairo for medical treatment. Passing through the main street, he noticed a big gathering, from which the booming voice of the shaykh sounded familiar. As he drew closer to it, he realised the voice was, of course, his student, Salih. Shaykh Muhammad smiled and sat down amongst the group of students. Shaykh Salih quickly spotted his old teacher from Dongola but continued his lesson. This was the ideal etiquette to show a teacher in his class. When he was finished, Shaykh Salih instructed all his students to greet and kiss the hands of Shaykh Muhammad. When Shaykh Salih belatedly met his teacher, Shaykh Muhammad said to him: *"Welcome, our master."* Shaykh Salih was more embarrassed than ever, and he humbly kissed the hands of his master, welcoming him with love and affection.

Shaykh Salih had the privilege of performing the *Hajj* twenty-seven times. However, one *Hajj* was incredibly special, as it included an encounter with a very distinct individual. This took place in Mina, where Salih came across an intoxicated mystic. Trusting his instinct, he felt this was no ordinary person. After a while, he approached this mystic and asked him: *"Where can I find Khidr?"* After a moment, the mystic looked at him and responded: *"You will find him in the Rawda in Madinah."*

After the *Hajj*, Shaykh Salih went to Madinah, and while he was sitting near the *Rawda*, he noticed a handsome man. The man wore a yellow turban, and he soon approached Shaykh Salih, seeking permission to ask him a question. He asked: *"We have come here to offer our greetings to the Prophet ﷺ. Does he hear us?"* Shaykh Salih replied: *"Yes, indeed, he hears us."* He then asked another question: *"When we return to our homes, thousands of miles away, we offer greetings to the Prophet ﷺ and hold gatherings in his honour. Does he hear us from thousands of miles away?"* Shaykh Salih replied with conviction: *"Definitely! He hears you from here and can hear you from there. There is no doubt."* The man, delighted, said: *"May God put your heart at peace as you have put my heart at ease."* Saying these words, he departed, disappearing into the crowd.

Afterwards, Shaykh Salih had a dream in which he found himself aboard a boat that seemed to match Musa's description. Shaykh Salih looked into the horizon and spotted a handsome man waving at him from a great distance away. As they drew closer, he belatedly recognised the person. It was the man who wore a yellow turban and had just asked him questions. Shaykh Salih realised this was *Khidr*. For the uninitiated: *Khidr* plays a special role in Sufism. He has been given permission by God to pass on certain litanies to the masters in the chains of Sufism. The masters then transmit these litanies to their disciples in the order dictated by *Khidr*.

So, look at yourself: did you recite their litanies?
Or are you tied down by weights?

Shaykh Salih stayed committed to his litanies and would not go without completing them. His usual practice was to roam the courtyards of Al-Azhar bearing a thousand-bead rosary, reciting two thousand salawat every night before returning to bed. He knew the importance of the litanies and emphasised the necessity of keeping to them. The disciple must understand that whichever litany is given to him by the shaykh was passed down from the Prophet ﷺ. To neglect the litanies would mean turning one's back on the Prophet ﷺ and all the *awliya* in the order.

My Lord send blessings upon the beloved: Muhammad ﷺ.
And his grandsons, the chiefs, and the champions.

Qasidah Radeena

رَضِينَا يَا بَنِي الزَّهْرَا رَضِينَا بِحُبٍّ فِيكُمُوا يُرْضِي نَبِينَا

We are most content, O sons of Al-Zahra,
most pleased, With a love of you that delights our Prophet ﷺ

رَضِينَا بِالنَّبِيِّ لَنَا إِمَامًا وَأَنْتُمْ آلُهُ وَبِكُمْ رَضِينَا

We are most satisfied with the Prophet ﷺ as our Imam,
And you are his family, and we are delighted with you

وَبِالسِّبْطِ الْحُسَيْنِ كَذَا أَخُوهُ وَحَيْدَرُ ثُمَّ زَيْنُ الْعَابِدِينَا

With Al-Husayn and with his brother,
With Haydar (Ali) and Zayn Al-Abidin

وَزَيْنَبُ مَنْ لَهَا فَضْلٌ سَمِيٌّ سُلَالَةُ أَحْمَدٍ فِي الطَّيِّبِينَا

And Zaynab of the highest virtue,
From Ahmad's pure descendants

لَهَا نُورٌ يُضِيءُ كَمِثْلِ شَمْسٍ مِنَ الْمُخْتَارِ نَشْهَدُهُ مُبِينَا

She has a light that shines like the Sun,

From the Chosen One, we see it clearly

لَهَا جُودٌ لَهَا كَرَمٌ وعَطْفٌ حَوَتْ فَضْلاً يُرَى لِلْمُنْصِفِينَا

She has generosity and compassion,

And virtues apparent to those who are fair

أَمِيرُ الْمُؤْمِنِينَ أَبُوكِ حَقًّا عَلِيٌّ سَادَ جَيْشَ الْعَارِفِينَا

Your father is truly the Commander of the Faithful, Ali,

master of the army of the Gnostics

وأُمُّكِ بَضْعَةُ الْمُخْتَارِ طَهَ مُحَبَّةٌ إِلَى الْهَادِي نَبِينَا

And your mother is a part of the Chosen One: Taha,

Most beloved to the guide, our Prophet ﷺ

وَكَانَ الْمُصْطَفَى يَحْنُو عَلَيْهَا حُنُوَّ مَوَدَّةٍ عَطْفًا وَلِينَا

Mustafa used to treat her most tenderly,

With love, compassion and softness

إِذَا اشْتَقْنَا إِلَى خَيْرِ الْبَرَايَا أَتَيْنَاكُمْ مُشَاةً رَاكِبِينَا

Whenever we long for the Best of Creation,

We come to you riding or on foot

فَأَنْتُمْ مِنْهُ بِالْأَسْرَارِ جِئْتُمْ وَجِئْنَاكُمْ فَشَاهَدْنَا الْأَمِينَا

For you came with his secrets,

And when we come to you, we see him!

*"So, look at yourself:
did you recite
their litanies?
Or are you tied down
by weights?"*

Salih Al-Jafari

الحق

The Absolute Truth

SUFISM

Javad Nurbakhsh (1926–2008)

I have been somewhat familiar with the writings of Dr Nurbakhsh. However, I never met him. I met some of his devotees during my B.A. degree at the University of Manchester (1991–1995). Saqib, Majid and Saheed wrote the original article in 2016.

> *Today, Sufism is a name without a reality.*
> *It was once a reality without a name.*

The Muslim world today is engulfed in confusion. An increasingly divisive breed of politics shapes its societies, and a set of viral, fundamentalist ideologies plague its youth. Modernity has depreciated traditional cultures in the east and the west, with too little or no significant opposition. Likewise, Sufism's perspective is considered an obsolete paradigm, emblematic of an era that modernity typifies as misguided and backwards. Along with the rise of socio-economic modernity in Muslim countries, Sufism can blame its marginal status on the bigoted screeds of many ultra-conservative groups - some countries have even seen wholesale crackdowns on Sufis, and their places of worship, by agencies of the present governmental regime.

Sufism is now quite often associated with the notion that it has 'detached itself from mainstream Islam to place a lesser emphasis on the tenets of *Shariah*.'

It has been endlessly stereotyped and attacked for its foremost 'vices' - be it idleness, begging, anti-social behaviour, ritualistic mysticism or the strange claim that as a philosophy, it only appeals to the ignorant masses. In the very same countries that once shunned it, it is once more taking root. Many Sufi lodges have reopened, and the *dhikr* gatherings are once again in full swing. More so than ever, Sufism requires a grand popular revival so that Muslims worldwide can reconnect with their discarded heritage.

In recent times, the esteemed Dr Nurbakhsh has promoted a brand of Sufism that has captured many hearts, endearing the creed to Muslim and non-Muslim alike. At first, he was just known as the master of the *Nimatullahi Sufi Order* – an outspoken opponent of the supposed incompatibility of modernity and Sufism. On the topic, he has commented: *"Contemporary culture is focused on materialism, on the love of money and material things. Humanity has completely forgotten the truth. Sufism can help remind people of the importance of loving and caring for others. By doing so, it can help to create love and peace among the different nationalities of the world."* Throughout his lifetime, he devotedly promoted the classical path of Sufism. Dr Nurbakhsh wrote and published many works on Sufism, including biographies of the masters of the path and primers on the *Nimatullahi Sufi Order's* principles.

Dr Nurbakhsh sponsored numerous international conferences and seminars to promote Sufism across the globe. He publically defined Sufism as a spiritual journey towards God - a journey from one's ego towards the truth. Of course, Sufism can be interpreted in many ways, so it is important to appreciate from the outset that no clear, official definition of Sufism exists (or can exist). Yet, this nebulous nature allows for thousands of interpretations, with each understanding depending on the individual. Indeed, Sufism has existed, we might say, since the beginning of mankind. The first Sufi was the Prophet ﷺ Adam, who was given the title *Safi Allah*. He spent his time on Earth seeking a connection with God, seeking forgiveness and attempting to make the journey back to his Lord. We follow in his footsteps.

Many prophets of the faith were known to wear *'suf'* (wool) to signify humility. Thus, the early Sufis also adopted this practice. For this reason, the most widely accepted origin of the word 'Sufi' stems from the Arabic word *'suf'* (wool). However, since there is no confirmed proof of the word's origin, another possibility is that the title was derived from *'Ahl Al-Suffa'* (People of the Bench): the seventy-two special Companions who lived close to the Prophet ﷺ . In a few sources, it is also mentioned that the word Sufi may derive from the Arabic word *'safa'* (purity) and that people were given the title 'Sufi' to compliment the purity of their hearts. A popular theory posits that the word originates from Western scholars' Greek word 'Sophia' (wisdom). It could be said that the significance of this openness, this ambiguity in the very interpretation of the word Sufi, is in itself the best reflection of what Sufism embodies.

If I can try to put it most simply, Sufism means to practice Islam with sincerity. Specifically, it means to adhere to the three dimensions that Jibril came down to teach us: Islam, faith and *Ihsan* (perfection). This third stage is often neglected by the most ignorant mass of people; it denotes the act of worshipping God as if you are seeing Him right before you. Overall, Sufism stands for a holistic spiritual progress along all three dimensions to accomplish a permanent personal state of devotion. Hujwiri (1009–1077) mentions that the Prophet ﷺ once asked of Haritha: *'What is the reality of your Iman?'* Haritha replied: *"I have cut off from this world. Its gold and silver and its clay are now equal in my sight. I pass my nights in wakefulness and my days in thirst. I will do this until I see the Throne of my Lord manifest and the people of paradise visiting one another and the people of hell wrestling with one another."* The Prophet ﷺ replied: *"You know. So, be steadfast."*

Born in the Kerman province of Iran, Javad was the son of Asadullah and Khanum Bibi. His grandfather, Hassan, apparently became entranced by his radiant eyes and beautiful smile when he was born. Thus he quickly became his grandfather's favourite. Hassan spent many hours in the company of young Javad. It was soon obvious to him that this young child had an inquisitive nature and a sheer intelligence far beyond his years. He sensed already that his grandson was destined to live a remarkable life. After Javad turned five, Asadullah enrolled him at the local *madrasa* to learn the Qur'an. To the surprise of his family and teachers, Javad progressed so rapidly over his first nine months that he was placed with a group of older children. The young boys were taught about Hafiz's Persian poetry to improve their literacy skills in this class. At times, Javad's inquisitive mind would suddenly land him in trouble as some of his teachers even complained about constantly being asked challenging complex questions by the young man.

When he reached seventh grade, his passion for poetry led him to start composing his own verses. One of his teachers praised his potential, saying: *"Javad is incapable of containing his untamed, wild spirit, which is why he is so restless. He has skipped a few grades and now finds himself among the older students. Still, he remains unsatisfied and continues to seek something else. Whatever that something may be, he will never find satisfaction until he attains it."* By his last year of high school, Javad aspired to study law or medicine at Tehran University. He shared his thoughts with his father, who was stunned: *"Are you crazy? Only a few people from around the entire country are accepted each year. You speak to me with full confidence that you will not only be accepted but that you'll have a choice in whether to qualify in law or medicine. We will just have to see if you pass the entrance exams - only then can this matter be taken seriously."*

Javad sat the entrance exams in the following year. As he had expected, he easily earned his entrance to the university. During this period, spurred on by his passion for poetry, he began a deep reading of Rumi's Mathnawi, which ignited a desire within his soul to pursue the study of Sufism. He found himself constantly fantasizing about visiting the lodge of his great ancestor, Shaykh Kamaluddin - a well-known Sufi in his time. He had occasionally heard his grandfather and father converse about the lodge, happily recounting many tales of their ancestor and admiring his devotion to the Sufi path. Javad's father gave him permission to visit the lodge, offering a few brief details on its location – too brief, as Javad found out. He became disheartened that no one he talked to seemed to know anything about its whereabouts. Finally, after hours of searching, he stumbled upon a derelict building surrounded by garbage. He now understood why the locals had no knowledge about the lodge – a sad victim of lasting neglect. At that moment of discovery, he felt his heart stir. Standing tall amongst the ruins, he made a pledge to himself that after he had finished his education and found a job, he would return to renovate this lodge in memory of Shaykh Kamaluddin.

Upon returning from this visit, Javad's behaviour was never the same. Whereas before, he often enjoyed the company of others, now he preferred to remain alone in solitude, spending his spare time in meditation. His parents were soon alarmed by his conduct and demeanour. His father even sought counsel from a Sufi friend, who advised him that Javad should visit Sayyidi Murshidi - a shaykh of the Nimatullahi Order who lived in Kerman. Javad obeyed and, during this visit, Sayyidi Murshidi asked him: *"Does your heart want to step upon the path to God? To the truth?"* Javad immediately replied: *"Yes."* He was initiated into the Nimatullahi Order that very day.

After this watershed, Javad experienced a series of intense spiritual states that began to affect his appearance. It was apparent to all that he was not eating and sleeping much. This, again, alarmed his parents. Asadullah visited Sayyidi Murshidi and complained that Javad was fast approaching the threshold of madness. He was about to throw away his entire life. Sayyidi Murshidi reassured Asadullah that his son would be fine. He assured him that Javad would one day bring great honour to his family as a Sufi. Sayyidi Murshidi then met with Javad and told him: *"I am aware of the burning in your heart. You no longer know the difference between day and night. You have travelled a long way in such a short time and have amazed me. You should be aware that the state you are now experiencing is the state of 'seeking'. However, you have upset your parents, and such is not the way of the Sufi. Be calm rather than hasty, for this path cannot be travelled without patience. Soon, you will go to Tehran to attend university. There you will have the opportunity to enjoy the companionship of our beloved master. For now, you must remain calm and patient. Without these qualities, you will never be able to continue this journey to the end."*

Javad heeded Sayyidi Murshidi's words. Eventually, the moment arrived for Javad to embark on the six-hundred-mile journey to reach Tehran – a distance he vanquished in just three days. Upon his arrival, he quickly made a friend, who helped him to find suitable accommodation. He registered for exams in law and medicine and was, indeed, successfully accepted by both departments. His final choice (medicine) was based on his reasoning that it would give him as many years as possible with a master who resided in Tehran. He wrote to his family, knowing his father would be delighted to hear all of this. Javad then travelled to the Tehran lodge, where the master of the Nimatullahi Order, Shaykh Munis Ali Shah, resided at the time. He gave a letter to the doorkeeper that had been addressed to the master by Sayyidi Murshidi. After reading it, Shaykh Munis Ali Shah asked a Darwish to set up Javad's accommodation and exam-entrance arrangements. Until now, Javad had remained silent. After asking permission to speak, he offered the shaykh an apology for not coming to the lodge sooner. He explained that this was to make all the necessary logistical arrangements to not burden anyone. Javad then added: *"My only wish now is to be able to serve you."* Shaykh Munis Ali Shah remained silent for a long time. Finally, he mentioned: *"There are two gatherings a week at the khanaqah (lodge); on a Thursday and a Sunday evening. You should attend and also partake in the simple meal."*

Over the next few months, Javad attended the lodge regularly. During one meeting with Shaykh Munis Ali Shah, Javad was given spare keys to the library and the lodge's front door. He was now totally responsible for the library and could come and go whenever he wished. So, Javad's entire life became dedicated to attending the lodge. He simultaneously indexed all the books in the library and continued his studies at the university. It soon became apparent to all that Shaykh Munis Ali Shah was already very fond of young Javad. The shaykh began to teach him Arabic so that he could access essential texts on Sufism. And the master gave Javad further responsibilities, including making sure all preparations were done for the weekly dinner on a Thursday night and managing all the lodge's financial affairs.

A Darwish once asked Javad to assist him with a complicated problem. Javad did so by visiting the Finance Ministry and quickly resolving the matter satisfactorily. A young finance official met Javad in this transaction and soon started experiencing sudden changes in his state of mind where he could no longer concentrate on his work. This effect bewildered him, as their discussion had been brief and centred on resolving the Darwish's problems. The official decided to arrange to meet with Javad again at the lodge. Over the next few weeks, their meetings became frequent. One day, the official surprised Javad by asking him if he could become his disciple, even though he had always aspired to become one of Shaykh Munis Ali Shah's followers. Nonetheless, he said he only sought initiation at Javad's hands and not the master. Javad did not respond, and he retreated to his room.

When Shaykh Munis Ali Shah came to perform prayers with him, Javad narrated what had just unfolded. Shaykh Munis Ali Shah beamed, and he immediately gave an astonished Javad his permission to initiate the young official. Shaykh Munis Ali Shah told him: *"You should be grateful. Such loyal people are rare in this world; he will be a sincere devotee and a loyal friend."* Hassan Kobari was indeed a loyal friend to Javad. He devoted himself wholeheartedly to the Sufi path for twenty-five years, right up to his death in 1978. During his master's lifetime, Javad would initiate only one other devotee - Hajii Muhammad. The approval of these initiations indicated the stature Javad held in his master's eyes. One night, Javad was awoken by a Darwish, who asked him to rush to the master's room.

Shaykh Munis Ali Shah had already been suffering from prostate trouble for some time. Following a brief examination, Javad diagnosed that the master had a urinary tract infection. This needed to be dealt with immediately, or it would become life-threatening. Javad quickly made enquiries for a doctor to visit. With it being so late, a doctor couldn't be found to come to the lodge. Just a fourth-year medical student at the time, Javad knew then that he had no choice but to do the operation himself. He slipped off to the nearest hospital and gathered all the appropriate surgical equipment. And, after asking his master's permission, he somehow completed the procedure successfully. There were no complications, and only a small amount of blood was spilt, no more than expected.

Some devotees had begun to grow jealous of Javad, resenting his closeness to the master. They now saw this as an opportune moment to cause mischief. One of them suggested that the minor spillage of blood was an indication that the inexperienced Javad had cunningly tried to kill the master under the cloak of saving him. These devotees called on a qualified physician to complete a full, objective examination of the master. Javad was also summoned to this appointment. After examining the master, the doctor remarked to him, *"What kind of Sufis are you? If it was not for this young man, the master might have died last night. You should be thanking him, not accusing him of harm."* Shaykh Munis Ali Shah remained quiet while this whole matter developed before his eyes. But suddenly, he stared daggers at the murids who had made the false accusation. Then, looking at Javad, he addressed him: *"Dr Nurbakhsh."*

After this, it became the norm for everyone at the lodge to refer to Javad as Dr Nurbakhsh. Later, the new Dr Nurbakhsh desired to sit a *chilla* (retreat), and so he sought permission from his master. Shaykh Munis Ali Shah addressed him again: *"Your everyday life consists of continual service to humanity, which is what truly matters on the path. Being responsible for all the affairs of the lodge, both material and spiritual, while still keeping up with your medical studies far surpasses the difficulty of a chilla."* However, the longing to complete a *chilla* would only burn brighter in Dr Nurbakhsh's heart. He wished to complete the *chilla* by adhering to the practice's strict rules and manners, as prescribed by the esteemed Shah Nimatullah Wali (1330–1431). Shaykh Munis Ali Shah was reluctant to allow him such an arduous *chilla*, fearing it would push Dr Nurbakhsh into madness. But Dr Nurbakhsh insisted to his master that he was aware of everything the *chilla* entailed. So, Shaykh Munis Ali Shah finally agreed. The *chilla* took place at the *Kerman Shah* lodge. When the forty days of the period had elapsed, Shaykh Munis Ali Shah arranged a celebration in Dr Nurbakhsh's honour. At the same time, a Darwish from the *Ahl-e-Haq Order* invited Dr Nurbakhsh to a special ceremony on behalf of his own master. As he attended the gathering the following day, he was informed that he was the only person outside of the *Ahl-e-Haq Order* to have ever been invited to such a ceremony.

After spending two months at the Kerman Shah lodge, Shaykh Munis Ali Shah returned to Tehran. He noticed that Dr Nurbakhsh was now spending all his time in the library and was no longer attending university. Upon inquiry, Dr Nurbakhsh informed his master: *"During our stay at the Kerman Shah lodge, the period for me to register for the final year of medical school elapsed. I will now have to wait until next year to register. I chose this degree because it was longer than many others, so I would have more time to serve you. It is through God's Grace that this period has been extended by a further year."* Shaykh Munis Ali Shah said to the other murids present: *"This Kirmani shaykh is vastly different to others. In but a short time, he has become ripe as old wine. Those of you who are truly serious about the path would do well to pay heed to him."* The following year, Dr Nurbakhsh completed his studies and was awarded his medical degree. Shaykh Munis Ali Shah quipped: *"Today, Dr Nurbakhsh has graduated from two academic and spiritual universities."* Later, Shaykh Munis Ali Shah informed Dr Nurbakhsh that the time had come for him to return to Kerman to practice medicine and serve people. Kerman was also an important area for the *Nimatullahi Order*. It was the burial place and end-point of many other masters' paths, including Shah

Nimatullah Wali.

One of Dr Nurbakhsh's major accomplishments was to write the biographies of the masters of the Nimatullahi Sufi Order. In this comprehensive work, he mentions that the Order traces its spiritual lineage back to Sayyiduna Ali through Hassan Al-Basri. Dr Nurbakhsh felt he held a strong personal connection with Shah Nimatullah Wali. So he founded the *Khanaqahi-Nimatullahi* publishing house in Tehran. Under his supervision, this press published over a hundred books on Sufism in Persian, along with reprints of most of Shah Nimatullah Wali's own writings. Dr Nurbakhsh viewed Shah Nimatullah Wali as the seminal reviver of classical Sufism in Iran. He had famously prohibited the use of hashish and opium when they were both in common use whilst also purging other non-Islamic elements that had crept into Sufism. Shah Nimatullah Wali insisted on the strictest adherence to the Shariah, believing that all people needed Sufism. He promoted the virtues of serving society and purifying the heart, which would clearly influence Dr Nurbakhsh in modern times.

Needless to say, Dr Nurbakhsh settled in Kerman. Shaykh Munis Ali Shah then wrote a letter addressed to his followers, announcing that Dr Nurbakhsh would be his eventual successor. He would not have long to wait. In June 1953, Dr Nurbakhsh was informed that his beloved master Shaykh Munis Ali Shah, had passed away. At twenty-six, Dr Nurbakhsh was now the master of the Nimatullahi Order, following Shah Nimatullah Wali's footsteps. His first act was to decree a code of behaviour that all Nimatullahi devotees were bound to observe. These included selfless service policies, contributions to society rather than mere seclusion, commitment to a public occupation, and strict adherence to the Shariah through the prohibition of hashish and opium.

As he assumed the responsibility of the Nimatullahi Order, only three *khanaqahs* actually existed. However, over the next two decades, the doctor would oversee the continual construction of nearly seventy lodges in Iran as his Order flourished and attracted many followers. He was assisted in their construction by the devotee, Mashallah Niktab. The first lodge that Mashallah Niktab was assigned to construct was that of Shaykh Kamaluddin. The pledge Dr Nurbakhsh had made as a young boy to his illustrious ancestor had now been fulfilled by its completion. Dr Nurbakhsh later commented: *"Niktab alone had to deal with all the troubles and hardships involved in the building of all of these lodges."*

Along with his responsibilities to the Order, Dr Nurbakhsh never neglected his occupational role as a licensed medical doctor. He even pursued his interest in medicine further, becoming a specialist in psychiatry, living in Paris and other foreign cities over long periods of scholarship. Here, he established lasting acquaintances with many western scholars interested in Sufism. In 1963, he was invited to deliver an insider's speech on Sufism by a leading western scholar called Professor Henry Corbin. Upon returning to Iran, he gained many academic promotions and eventually attained a professorship in the psychiatric faculty. He wrote and published many articles purely on psychiatry and established his own private psychiatric clinic adjacent to the Tehran lodge. Here, he primarily treated patients who were too poor to pay for their care. Many years later, Mashallah Niktab was told of the statement his master had made about his role in building the lodges. He immediately responded: *"None of it was trouble and hardship, none of it. It was all love. All love."*

In the early 1970s, several young American devotees travelled to Iran to meet Dr Nurbakhsh. Dr Nurbakhsh made his first trip to the USA following their initiation into the Order, touring across the country, and initiating seekers of the path in many great cities. Following this reception, Mashallah Niktab was sent to the USA with instructions to establish lodges. The first American lodge was opened in San Francisco. This was followed a year later with the first centre in New York City. With the initiation of devotees from Sufi groups in various countries, lodges were opened on almost every continent. This wholesale expansion led to Dr Nurbakhsh having his most important works translated into English to spread his wisdom to a wide western audience.

Following the Islamic revolution in Iran in 1979, Dr Nurbakhsh felt forced to migrate from his homeland to the United Kingdom, tragically unable to fulfil his life's goal of creating an International Centre for the study of Sufism. In his exile, he lived first in London and then in Oxfordshire, renting an area of farmland known locally as 'the Old Windmill'. It was here that the Nimatullahi Research Centre was first opened. The quarterly journal it spawned, Sufi, was first published in 1989. It continues to be published today, having reached its 90th edition. On Friday the 10th of October 2008, having been the master of the Nimatullahi Order for over half a century, Dr Nurbakhsh passed away in peace at the Old Windmill. He was survived by his wife and five children. His son, Alireza, succeeded him.

The life of Dr Nurbakhsh, as a seeker, disciple, shaykh and then master of the Order, stands out as the epitome of a Sufi who fully traversed the spiritual journey towards God. He is an example to us of all our potentials to escape the ego, move towards God, and live selflessly in service to humanity. He practised these principles all through his life. Being an itinerant Sufi amid modernity, he made Sufism culturally relevant so that a greater mass of people could aspire to live meaningful lives and do their own service to humanity. Dr Nurbakhsh once elaborated on the fundamental message of Sufism; *"To be a Sufi means to be in love with the truth - in other words, God. And for someone to love the truth, that person must love all human beings and serve them, regardless of their race, religion, or nationality. At the very minimum, being a Sufi means not disturbing or bothering anyone and tolerating without offence other people's disturbances and other people bothering you."* When asked to strictly define Sufism, Dr Nurbakhsh cracked: *"Whatever comes into words is not Sufism."*

*"To be a Sufi means
to be in love with
the Truth -
in other words, God."*

Dr Nurbakhsh ﷺ

The All Aware

SELFLESS SERVICE

Shukri Al-Luhafi (1920–2015)

During a visit to Damascus in 2007, I met Shaykh Shukri at a dhikr gathering. That brief encounter instilled in me a deep love for him and his practice. Later, one of his students gave me ijaza. Hence, the Shaykh became my grand teacher. Barkat and Zubair wrote the article in 2015.

Khidmah, noun: the action of helping or doing work for someone:
"A selfless act rendered without the pursuit of reward"
synonyms: an act of assistance · good turn · compassion · kindness ·
Active participant: *Khadim* (the doer of service)

Once upon a time, a woman worked as a presser for the royal family. Her main duty was to wash and iron the clothes of the princess. Obviously, these garments were made from the most expensive materials. One day, this lady's son spied and saw one of the princess's dresses and became overawed by its beauty. He enquired: *"Mother, to whom does this belong?" "My son, I have kept this secret hidden from you so far. Today, I will disclose it, but you must promise not to reveal it to anyone. I work for the royal family, and I have been assigned to look after the princess's clothes,"* replied the mother.

After hearing this, the son became keen to participate in this service to the royal family. He begged his mother if she would allow him to iron the princess's clothes. At first, the mother was hesitant, but his pleading persisted. She allowed her son to iron and fold the clothes under her guidance. When the clothes were returned to the princess, she noticed the difference in her folded clothes. She summoned the lady and informed her: *"You have been in our service for many years. However, only recently have my clothes been immaculately ironed and folded."*

The lady returned home, relieved. Subsequently, she continued to allow her son to iron and fold the clothes of the princess. The son gradually fell in love with the princess just by caring for her dresses, so he desired to see her. However, his mother refused, worrying such contact could endanger both their lives. She needn't have worried. Just after this, the son tragically contracted a fatal illness and died very suddenly. The mother, though grieving, had to resume the duty of ironing the princess's clothes. The princess now noticed a new difference in the standard of ironing and folding, and again she summoned the lady. This time, she was less than impressed. The lady refused to reveal the truth, but the princess persisted in her inquiry. Eventually, the mother told the princess of her whole ordeal and informed her that her son had sadly passed away. Though posthumous, the princess fell in love with the young man's devotion.

The Sufi masters use this brief tale as an allegory to illustrate how human beings should be like this young man, who cannot see the object of his desires - God. However, through servitude, mankind can come to know of God through serving His creation.

From the refuse collector to the woman in the jobcentre (and in fact, every living organism) performs some form of service. Though some may be more skilled than others, everyone is still performing a service. If you are not, then you can be considered 'out-of-service'. Of course, this concept of service has been propagated and encouraged in every faith and through nearly all walks of life. Even many of those who choose not to believe in God still say they believe in benefiting others. If we were to observe the corporate world, we would note how companies spend billions of pounds a year to train their employees to provide the right form of courteous service. They follow and promote the notion that one satisfied customer could bring many more potential customers. Such an example, however, is still a form of service to the world. Whether it is the sales rep giving a discount to a loyal customer or an old woman setting up a monthly direct debit with Oxfam, these are all instances of standard service, contributing to an idea of helping others. As Muslims, we believe in a Lord that has created us for a purpose. In the Qur'an, God mentions: *"Those who remember God while standing or sitting or [lying] on their sides, give thought to the creation of the heavens and the earth, [saying], 'Our Lord, You did not create this aimlessly; exalted are You [above such a thing]; then protect us from the punishment of the Fire.'"* (3:191)

It is our belief that God has ordained for all things an individual purpose. Some of these He has made manifest to us already, and others He still hides from us. However, from the beginning, God made explicitly known the purpose of man and *jinn* alike in the Qur'an; *"And I did not create the jinn and mankind except to worship Me."* (51:56). The term 'worship' is a highly interpretable word, and there are many different forms of it as a practice. One of the many forms of worship that we often do not appreciate, is the general call for us to live in servitude to God's creation. Despite the worldly rank one may hold, all human beings are, at their essence, servants of God and His creation.

Some charge for their services while others go unpaid. Amongst those who do not take payments are our mothers. Shaykh Nazim Al-Haqqani often stated: *"If I were the ruler or president of my time, I would pay the women double the wage of the man [due to their work in the household]"*. It is this selfless service that mothers do on an unceasing basis that always goes unnoticed. Yet they continue to work tirelessly to feed, clothe and provide for their families without any desire for immediate reward. Therefore, the mother is considered the primary and foremost station of service. It is from your mother that you first learn how to serve.

We have thus established that there are two types of service:

i) Service for worldly gain.

ii) Service for the pleasure of God.

Any type of service can be fitted into one of the two categories mentioned above, even seemingly insignificant chores or tasks. For example, suppose one earns a livelihood by *halal* means and does so intending to seek God's pleasure. In that case, this can be considered a service to God and rewarded accordingly. Service done without the pursuit of reward can also win the hearts of men. If a child does service to his parents, then they will bless and pray for him. If a student does something for his teacher, or a disciple does something for his master, they will bless him likewise. When we show signs of our potential to carry out sincere service, then God sends us guides and teachers. Their task is to transform us from weak servants into strong servants. By bettering ourselves and following our teachers' guidance, God bestows us with ever-increasing opportunities to serve His creation.

But why is serving God's creation so important? The great poet of Pakistan, Allama Iqbal, explains it this way: *"There are many people that want to be servants of God, but I am looking for the servants of God to serve them."* This is how you reach God; by serving His creation.

Like all else in our faith, this concept starts with the Prophet ﷺ. To serve the needy and oppressed is indeed a prophetic quality. Our beloved Prophet ﷺ taught us to be considerate and gentle with all creatures. His major concern in life was to serve humanity. It would sadden him if anyone around him were in distress, even a mere animal. The Prophet ﷺ once entered the garden of a man from the Ansar, and, upon seeing him arrive, a camel started crying. The camel complained to the Prophet ﷺ that his owner starved it and tired it out through overwork. The Prophet ﷺ took pity on it, and informed it's owner not to overburden the poor animal. Likewise, there are numerous such examples of the Prophet's ﷺ love, care and affection for God's creatures. Even in his home, he was known to do all the household chores himself, like milking the goats, sewing his own clothes and kneading the flour. He never saw any activity as self-denigrating or in any way beneath him. As he taught the ummah: any action done with good intentions becomes a form of service.

Through the blessed example of the Prophet ﷺ, his beloved Companions also learnt to perform sincere acts of service through emulating him. When the Prophet ﷺ saw his Companions' development, he would entrust them with different, suitable responsibilities. For example, Bilal was given the duties of giving the call to prayer and collecting donations from the public for special occasions. He was considered a trustworthy and noble person. However, not all Companions were given such an exclusive right. Each was given their service according to their capacity and ability.

We should be aware by now that service is a profound aspect of spirituality. A student serves his master, and once his service has been accepted, he himself becomes a master. Traditionally, a teacher would have students who would serve him - not because they had been indentured or enslaved but rather because their love and admiration for him as a person urged them to please their teacher's heart by performing regular service to him or his family.

Shaykh Sa'di (1210–1292) explains: *"The spiritual path of Sufism is not having a prayer mat, a rosary or a nice cloak; this does not make you a Sufi. What makes you a Sufi is service to the people."* Once an individual has been through the necessary training with his master, he will achieve the true status of servanthood. As his service grows and diversifies, he will advance through the spiritual stages until he becomes intimate with God. This nearness will enable the khadim to taste the many benefits of servitude. Following this, God will bestow him with abundant opportunities to provide myriad forms of service to His creation. But what does all this service require of a servant?

First and foremost, the *khadim* must always understand that all opportunities to serve are divine favours from God. He must ensure that he is present in every action and train himself to avoid any feelings of pride. He must understand that his service on Earth is the rent he pays for his room in paradise. When true sincerity complements his actions, then the *khadim* will dismiss the search for any physical rewards.

Secondly, the *khadim* must stay consistent in every act of service. He cannot 'choose' to do service when it suits him. Rather, he lives on the lookout for those in need of help and service. The quality of steadfastness is closely tied to sincerity here, as you cannot be consistent in any of your actions without it.

Moreover, the *khadim* must look through the lens of mercy when dealing with all people. He must be compassionate in his approach. Otherwise, he risks being needlessly harsh or abrupt with people who may be suffering in delicate situations. The *khadim* must also possess and share a skill or talent. The more skills or talents that one acquires, the more he can benefit other people. For instance, if a person possesses a mechanical knack, he can use it to assist a person whose car may have broken down. Conversely, if a person is approached for help and cannot offer any assistance, this can be a deep embarrassment.

Another key component of true service is the compulsion to perform every act with love. Without love, the *khadim* may treat any particular act as a chore or a menial task. Only through love will he find himself able to place someone else's needs before his own. Such love should make it impossible for him to ever tire from doing service. With it, he will receive the divine sources of energy that will enable him to endure great difficulties. This outcome is illustrated particularly well in this narrative.

In addition to all of the above, the *khadim* must remain in a constant state of awareness. This enables him to notice the opportunities and occasions in life that require his service. If he fails to achieve this state, then serving opportunities will pass him by, and he may come to rue his complacency.

The seventh key element of true service is selflessness and voluntarism. When a person carries out a service solely for the sake of God; this is what we deem to be 'selfless'. This is the essential quality for your acts to be accepted in the eyes of God. Amir Ismail Samani (849–907) was known to emerge from his palace during the extremes of winter just to listen to the plight and requests of his people. His courtiers would advise him to get this work over with during the summer to not expose himself to such harsh weather. However, he would always refuse, stating: *"This is the most crucial time of the year. This is when people are facing the most hardships, this is when they need me the most."* And so, he would stand out in the street all day, fulfilling the requests and needs of the people. Upon finishing a shift, he would give two cycles of prayer of thankfulness and then reflect before God. He would state aloud: *"O God, You made this day so blessed for me. You allowed me to serve Your people, and for this, I am eternally grateful."*

The eighth, but arguably the most important key to performing sincere service is that the khadim must always remain humble. Without humility, his ego will prevent him from aiding or assisting anyone. The true servant will not see any form of service as being demeaning or degrading. Rather, he will always see it as an unmissable opportunity from God.

All of the qualities mentioned above were epitomised by one individual who lived in our time: Shaykh Shukri Al-Luhafi. He was born in Damascus in 1920, and his father was a shoemaker – a kind, tolerant and generous person. Shukri's mother came from Algeria and was especially pious. As a young boy, Shukri went to school, and by the age of nine, he had started memorising the Qur'an. After completing his school years in 1944, he continued his higher education in the faculty of Shariah at the University of Damascus. Later, Shukri would teach widely in various schools in Aleppo, Dara, and Damascus. He eventually became a principal in the Ashrafiyya School in his hometown. His life was spent in the full service of education. However, despite working as a teacher, his best student was always himself. He learnt other languages, such as French and Persian, so well that he was deemed competent enough to teach them. He also perfected one of the noblest arts in Islam: calligraphy. A skill so revered that Ali once said: *"If you learn calligraphy, you will never starve."* At home, Shukri was married to a noble lady from the Prophet's ﷺ family. They were blessed with four children.

The Qur'an can be recited in ten different ways, called *Qira'ats*. Shukri learned all ten. Each *Qira't* requires precise knowledge and basically constitutes its own science. Shukri gathered this knowledge from Shaykh Yusuf Abu Dayl and received the ijaza from Shaykh Al-Kurdiz. And so, despite being a husband and then later a father and teacher, he perpetually benefitted from the wisest spiritual leaders around him.

Shaykh Shukri's spiritual heritage came from being a Shadhili. His shaykh was Shaykh Abdur Rahman Al-Shaghuri (1912–2004). However, Shukri's first shaykh was Muhammed Al-Hashimi (1881–1961). Shaykh Al-Hashimi, during his lifetime, was a very prominent saint in Damascus, and many people benefited from his influence. Shukri's mannerisms and characteristics even came to remind people of his shaykh. Like his shaykh, Shukri would go to the market outside the mosque and pick up any food people had thrown away. His shaykh was also renowned for taking the trouble to arrange people's shoes in the mosque - another service that Shukri emulated from his master and consistently practised.

However, Shukri's greatest service was to give water to the people who attended the Shadhili hadra gathering in the mosque. This had been his constant duty since the 1960s. Even when he was over ninety years old, he could not be relieved from it. Physically, Shukri was small, and he aided this stature by constantly looking down in humility. He did this all his life. People would say that he reminded them of the Prophet's ﷺ Companions. He carried himself like he was from another age. He had no interest in wealth or any earthly position.

The people who saw him regularly never saw him wear anything apart from the same two or three different sets of clothes. His focus was solely on God, and he exhausted all his energies in service to God's creation. Whether creation showed itself in the form of students or the general public that had just wandered into the mosque, he set out to serve them in any and every gathering. Many people valued his company, and one of them later remarked: "[Shayk Shukri] is very poor, yet so content with his life. Due to his age, he has difficulties trying to stand up or even walk, but for us, he goes all the way to the shops to buy us food."

As we have seen, *khidmah* is not just a mere service. It is a practice exemplified by the life of Shaykh Shukri. As we have listed: he was an expert in Persian and French. He mastered ten different Qur'an recitations, poetry and jurisprudence and calligraphy. He chose the path of service. He was offered a high spiritual rank and the chance to leave the service to move on to a place where he would serve as a master like those before him. Yet, he refused every offer and honour just so he could remain a *khadim*. He truly understood that to be a *khadim* is the greatest honour for any human being. At an age where most people sit back hoping to be served, here was an individual who would serve water as if he was an adolescent doing his part for his community's happiness. And people who knew him noted that this individual was an *abdal* and the leader amongst them.

To understand Shaykh Shukri's reputation for service, we need to understand the following account:

As a young man, Faqir Muhammad, was involved in an accident and broke his leg. He was brought to Mirpur for treatment. It was here that he came to know of Qibla Alam. Once he had met Qibla Alam, he decided to devote the rest of his life to his service. Even after Qibla Alam passed away, he still stayed in his family's service. Hadrat Sahib narrates how this loyal and true servant died: *"I visited him in his last moments, and I asked him, 'You have served your shaykh and his family all your life. What have you gained from all your service?' Faqir*

Muhammad replied, *'I do not regret anything in my life. My shaykh is standing in front of me, welcoming me into the next life. Therefore I am content'."*

Soon after saying this, Faqir Muhammad passed away with a smile on his face.

"A life worth living and a life worth dying for is the life of a true servant."

Shukri Al-Luhafi

الودود

The Most Loving

MOTHER

Nizamuddin Awliya (1238–1325)

Shaykh Nizamuddin is one of my most beloved Sufi saints. I visited his grave in 1980. I often cite him in my gatherings. His teachings always feel fresh to me, and I never tire of talking or writing about him. I even named my second daughter after him. Sayyid Amjid wrote the original article in 2015.

A man once came to the Prophet ﷺ, seeking his permission to participate in *Jihad*. The Prophet ﷺ asked him if his mother was alive. He replied in the affirmative. The Prophet ﷺ told him to serve his mother as paradise lay at her feet.

Once, a group of Companions came to inform the Prophet ﷺ that a dying man was struggling to utter the creed. The Prophet ﷺ went to the man's house and told him to recite it. He cried in reply: *"O Messenger of God ﷺ, I am trying, but the words are not coming onto my tongue."* The Prophet ﷺ told his Companions to bring in his mother. When she entered, she was asked what sin her son had committed. She replied: *"My son became disobedient, and he no longer cared for me. I cannot forgive him for the pain and suffering he has left me in my old age."* The Prophet ﷺ told her that unless she forgave her son, the earth would not accept him, and he would have to be burnt instead of being buried. She cried: *"O Messenger of God ﷺ, he is my flesh and blood! I cannot bear to see my son being burnt.”* The Prophet ﷺ replied that if she did not forgive her son, he would inevitably burn forever in the depths of hell. So she did forgive him, and he managed to utter the creed before death.

The Arabic word for mother, *umm*, depicts her as 'the source'. She is the foundation from which a child begins to learn and develop. A mother is usually the first and foremost institution that nurtures a child, shaping its character by imparting knowledge, skills, etiquettes, and conduct. It is her beliefs, values, and mannerisms that the child adopts from the onset of life. Therefore, a righteous and upright mother will naturally produce children who live up to high morals and standards. Many great people have received the compliment throughout history: *“Blessed be the mother that bore you.”* This connection implies that the credit of their accomplishments ultimately and undeniably lies with their mother. She is the one who brought the great ones into this world and the one who raised them. God knows this and has raised the mother's rank to be three times greater than the father. He has granted mothers immense love for their children. All of the Generous Souls who have attained nearness to God have strong connections with their mothers.

Sayyid Muhammad, known as Nizamuddin, was born in 1238 in Badayoun, India. His lineage can be traced back to Imam Husayn. His ancestors originally migrated from Bukhara to Lahore before moving to Badayoun. His father, Sayyid Ahmad, and his mother, Sayyidah Zulaykha, were notably pious people. Sayyid Ahmad was himself a great saint and a scholar. The Sultan pleaded with Sayyid Ahmad to take up a position as a judge. And he accepted, but only for a short period before retiring into seclusion. Sayyidah Zulaykha once had a dream in which she had to choose whose life to spare between her husband and her son. Out of love and compassion, she chose her son. Sayyid Muhammad was five years old when his father died. Thus leaving his mother to bear the responsibility for raising both of their children on her own. Although she was from a wealthy family, she refused to accept any assistance from her kin after her husband's death. She remained resolute in fulfilling her responsibilities while maintaining her late husband's dignity and honour. But this was still the most difficult period in her life. She held firm to her principles and kept absolute trust in her Lord. Whenever she was faced with a particularly difficult situation, she would hold out the hem of her blouse. She'd then recite *salawat* on the Prophet ﷺ five hundred times before making her plea to God. And whenever she did this, her prayers were answered.

Sayyidah Zulaykha always did her utmost to provide for her children. Nevertheless, in unavoidable circumstances, they would sometimes go without food for many days. Whenever this happened, she would say to her eldest: *"Nizam, my son, today we are God's guests."* One day he asked her what the phrase meant. She replied: *"When we have nothing to eat, then we say that we are God's guests. God sends us food for our souls, which sparks light and contentment in our hearts."*

Sayyid Muhammad eventually became a student at the local *madrasa*. His mother instructed him to always remain discreet about his family's poverty. When there was no food at home, he was told to keep away from the other students during lunchtime. He had one classmate who happened to be the son of the local police inspector. Thus, every day, servants brought lunch for him. One day, this boy stumbled on Sayyid Muhammad sitting alone. The boy offered to share his excess food with him, but he steadfastly refused. That evening he mentioned this to his mother, who took him in her arms and told him: *"My son, you are a Sayyid. A Sayyid is patient when he is hungry and, when he has food, gives it to the poor. When he has clothes, he gives them to those in need."*

The next day, the same thing happened. Each day his mother would say that they were God's guests. This gave Sayyid Muhammad patience and courage as he reflected on the meaning behind the words. The same boy found him sitting quietly at lunchtime and still insisted that he share his food on the third day. Sayyid Muhammad began to cry when the boy mentioned that his mother had made him a particularly special sweet dish. The boy asked him why he was crying, and Sayyid Muhammed confessed that his mother used to make a sweet dish when his father was alive. After much persistence, Sayyid Muhammad ate, and, for the rest of the day, he felt guilty. He blamed himself for having eaten while his mother and sister remained hungry at home. When he returned that evening, he fell at his mother's feet crying, and he confessed what he had done. Sayyidah Zulaykha kissed him, saying: *"My dear son, do not feel ashamed. God sent some food for us today as well. The maid was able to sell the wool that I had spun, and she bought some food. God willing, I will make a sweet dish, which you can take for your friend to repay his kindness."*

Some people arrived at the door with grain, butter, and many other food supplies as they were talking. They informed Sayyidah Zulaykha that the police inspector had sent these as gifts. However, she refused to accept them. Even after another round of cajoling, she refused and insisted on returning all the items. She then sat her children down and explained that although it was a blessed Sunnah to accept gifts, it was most likely that the inspector felt compelled to send these goods to them out of pity. His son had probably told him of his friend's plight. She said to them: *"I cannot accept offerings like this, as I do not want pity or charity. Since your father died, I have taken nothing from my parents or from any of my relatives. If I wanted anything, I could have asked them, they were wealthy and able to support me. Instead, I have strived to spend my life in patience and gratitude, earning a living by working. I have achieved this through hard work and reliance on God, not through gifts and favours. I have returned these things so that, tomorrow, your dignity and honour will not be compromised. Otherwise, it is likely that somewhere in his heart, your friend will think that he, or his father, has done you a favour. I do not want you to ever feel in debt to other people."*

She was eventually able to see the effects of this guidance upon her son, as illustrated by the following account:

One day, Sayyid Muhammad returned home from the madrasa when he saw many people gathered on the road. He approached the crowd and found out that a Hindu ruler had recently attacked a Muslim territory, looting wildly and killing women and children. In response, the Sultan had sent an army with a warrant to detain him. After being defeated, he was taken captive, along with his wife and son. The people had assembled to see the prisoners as they were in transit to the Sultan's court in Delhi. Sayyid Muhammad made his way through the people and saw an elegantly dressed woman and a boy standing beside her. He noticed that the boy was shivering in the cold, so he offered his shawl to him. The boy did not understand what Sayyid Muhammad was trying to do, and he swiftly hid behind his mother out of fear. Sayyid Muhammad asked someone to translate that he offered his shawl to protect the boy from the cold. The woman replied that, as the queen, she could not accept charity. He insisted that this was not charity but a gift. Eventually, she accepted the shawl and wrapped it around her son. Upon returning home, Sayyid Muhammad's mother noticed he was missing his shawl. When questioned, he informed her that he could not bear to see the boy shivering in the cold, and so he'd given it away. *"Well done, my son,"* she said, *"this is how a Sayyid should be. I pray that God makes you a remover of difficulties."*

It would be appropriate to learn more about Sayyid Muhammad's life from someone who heard about it directly from him. Amir was his dearest devotee, but Sayyid Muhammad confided in Khusrau (1253–1325) and talked at length about his childhood. *He writes: "In his old age, my master, Shaykh Nizamuddin, often mentioned his childhood and the precious moments he spent with his mother. He attributed many virtues to her. Seldom did he talk about her without crying; he still missed her dearly."* I often contemplated the relationship between a child and his mother. I realised that even the prophets held immense love and devotion towards their mothers. This relationship must be especially dear to God. I began to understand how God has placed this relationship in the hearts of those close to Him. After all, is it not so that even the Prophet ﷺ sought special permission from God to visit his mother's grave in later life? The Companions who accompanied this journey later reported: "He cried so much at her grave that we feared he would die." Shaykh Nizamuddin once told me about his mother's death. He spent his days studying in the mosque while his mother and sister lived in a small, rented house in Delhi. He visited her one evening. Upon sighting the new moon, he looked upon her face and made the traditional supplication. She smiled and sighed to him: "O Nizam, whose face will you look upon at the next moon?" Within a matter of days, she became ill, and her condition steadily deteriorated. I was in tears as he described her final moments: she looked at both of her children with love and compassion for the last time. She prayed to God for their well-being, and finally, she said, "I leave you in God's care." I cannot even begin to imagine the pain and anguish Shaykh Nizamuddin must have felt. His father had already died, leaving his mother to raise her children by herself. Then she, too, passed on, leaving him alone in this world. However, my master, Shaykh Nizamuddin, said that if his mother had left him an inheritance of chests overflowing with gold and silver, it would have been nothing compared to those final blessed words. He revealed that she had left him in God's care, and, without a doubt, this was the best gift she could have left him.

I cannot recall a single day when I did not hear Shaykh Nizamuddin mention his mother or pray for her. He once told me about how Bibi Nur and Bibi Hur – both friends of Sayyidah Zulaykha – had expressed how much they admired her nobility for miraculously raising her children with high morals and good values. They praised her, saying: "O dear Zulaykha, how blessed are you, who has a son that will pray for you after you die. How unfortunate are we that we have no one to remember us after our death?" She told her friends that she would ensure that her son visited their graves and prayed for them too, just as they would eventually be buried next to each other."

Shaykh Nizamuddin once said: "We did not drop out of the sky, but we were brought into this world by our mothers, who nourished and nurtured us to make us who we have become today." He acknowledged that his mother had endeavoured to instil good qualities in him. "However, the goodness that we do ourselves also influences our deceased parents. Our good deeds and acts of worship still benefit our mothers. If not for their guidance and upbringing, we would not have achieved our potential to engage in these good deeds. The characteristics we glean from our mothers during our childhood leave a permanent imprint on our personalities."

On another occasion, Shaykh Nizamuddin was ill and bedridden for many days, yet his concern remained for others. He mentioned that a stranger had visited him earlier that day, telling him: "O master, you receive without asking what is desired by kings and sultans. People offer you all kinds of gifts and show you great devotion and respect. Even the royals pay tribute to you and honour you. Indeed, you must not have a worry in the world." Shaykh Nizamuddin began to cry, saying that if only the man could have seen just how many people regularly came to him with their sufferings. "Had he realised the impact it has on me, the pain and anguish I endure, the heaviness that weighs on my heart, he would never have said this." He explained himself: "If I did not take this burden and did not worry for others, then how could I pray to God to remove these difficulties. People bring their problems to me with the hopes of attaining God's mercy. It becomes an obligation that I take these griefs upon myself. It is necessary to share their grief and to appreciate their predicaments. Taking the distress of so many people each day, how can it even be imagined that I do not have a worry in the world?"

Shaykh Nizamuddin ultimately accredited his compassion to his good upbringing. He attested that it was only through adopting his mother's etiquettes that signalled his path to enlightenment. He once said that meeting the blessed people of his life - from his first teacher to his shaykh, Baba Farid – had all followed from the respect, reverence, and good manners his mother had taught him. The great master Bayazid Al-Bastami once said that he had received more practical benefit from his mother than the three hundred masters he had served in search of spirituality. He quipped: "I found it in the place I most neglected; at the feet of my mother."

Blessed indeed is Nizamuddin's mother, who gave birth to a soul who is the source of so much comfort and relief. He is indeed our gateway to paradise for me and the millions of seekers who regularly pay tribute at his shrine.

Khusrau writes:

Every group has a faith, a direction to which they turn.
I turned my face towards the one with the tilted cap.

Shaykh Nizamuddin is deemed the most successful shaykh of the *Chishtiyya Order* in all its history. His deputies were dispatched throughout India, spreading his teachings and practices widely. They boil down to the classic imperative: to serve and look after others. In this way, he was able to directly influence the lives of millions of people. Khusrau states that our mothers have an important effect on forming our characteristics. So this correlates to them having a considerable stake in our actions and deeds. Shaykh Nizamuddin's success should and will always be ascribed to his mother. Thus, she is the true source of relief and benefit experienced by millions. Furthermore, the effects of this relationship bring rewards not just in this life but transcend into the Hereafter.

Today we can see that very few of us capitalise on every opportunity to serve and honour our mothers, as we often take their presence for granted. On the other hand, many of us have lost our mothers and can longer care for them again. Once, a person asked the Prophet ﷺ what action he could do to benefit his deceased mother. The Prophet ﷺ advised him that he could dig a well and dedicate it to her. In this manner, even in death, she would be rewarded whenever anyone would drink from it. The Prophet ﷺ recommended that they regularly visit their parents' graves, particularly on Fridays, to recite Surah Yasin and dedicate its reward to them. In response, one man asked what he should do if he didn't know where his parents were buried. The Prophet ﷺ advised him to draw a line on the ground and imagine it as his parents' graves.

The honour of the maternal bond is demonstrated by the recent example of a young man who went to Hajj. As he performed *tawaf* around the Ka'ba with his mother, she told him she wanted to kiss the well-known black stone. However, getting close to the Ka'ba itself was almost impossible, let alone the black stone. Nevertheless, he tried for her sake, and, on the first round, he managed to draw nearer to the Ka'ba. As the crowd jostled and pushed each other, he saw the way suddenly open. He pointed it out to her, and his mother could move through the space and kiss the stone without any difficulty. He then tried for himself but was only able to touch it with his hand. He continued making tawaf but couldn't stop himself from attempting it once more. He realised that his mother was indeed the *Hajr Al-Aswad* for him and more in a moment of inspiration. So, on each of the seven turns around the Ka'ba, he kissed his mother's hand instead, knowing what she meant to him.

Shaykh Nizamuddin achieved nearness to God through his service, honour and dedication to his mother. From an early age, he learnt and adopted several divine attributes and qualities from her. By holding firm to her teachings, he attained her pleasure and happiness. And consequently, her prayers were endorsed from above. For seven centuries, millions of people have continued to visit his shrine in Delhi; seeking his blessings and relief from their troubles, still considering him as their intercessor to God's mercy.

Khusrau narrates: *"I swear that I have witnessed the fulfilment of Sayyidah Zulaykha's prayer. Indeed, my master became the remover of difficulties. The poor and needy and the elite visited him seeking his intercession, blessings, and prayers. Ministers and even sultans strove to be allowed in his presence, as he was a patron for everyone. People from all walks of life, far and wide, travelled to him to empty their troubled hearts. Consequently, they found themselves liberated from the chains of their worries and afflictions. I believe that all this was the result of his mother's prayer during his childhood."*

"We did not drop out of the sky, but we were brought into this world by our mothers, who nourished and nurtured us to make us who we have become today."

Nizamuddin Awliya

The Uniter

MARRIAGE

Sayyidah Maymunah (594–673)

Sayyidah Maymunah is the last wife of the Prophet ﷺ. We have visited her grave on the outskirts of Makkah on numerous occasions. This article is written in a metafiction style in which fact and fiction are combined. However, all references to the people and events are correct. The question-answer technique is to create an affinity with the subject and the readers. Sayyid Amjid originally compiled the article in 2013.

"O the wives of the Prophet!
You are not like any other women." (33:32)

"Ya Ummi, what is the reason behind God proclaiming in the Qur'an that you and the rest of the noble wives of the Prophet ﷺ are unlike other women?"

"O my Son, this is a unique honour granted to us by the Lord of creation. He has distinguished us from the rest of humanity in His infinite wisdom and mercy. The Prophet ﷺ once said about us, "God selected my Companions." We are truly blessed for being selected from all of creation to accompany and support him. The Companions will have access to the Prophet ﷺ. However, we have been granted the honour to be his wives in paradise. Our relationship is forever and is not broken by death. It is for this reason that while other widows are permitted to re-marry, we

are forbidden to re-marry after the Prophet ﷺ as we will always remain his wives."

"Ya Ummi, just as prophethood was sealed with the Prophet ﷺ . As the last wife, you completed the noble qualities of the 'Mothers of the Faithful'. A Qur'anic verse was revealed, indicating God's acceptance of your marriage. Even Aishah has described you as the most considerate and mindful of all relationships. She said: "She is the most pious amongst us and the kindest to kith and kin."

"O my son, every one of the Mothers of the Faithful, possesses noble qualities. Khadijah was great support for the Prophet ﷺ during the early period in Islam. Moreover, the noble lineage of the Prophet ﷺ continues through her blessed children. Likewise, each wife had unique characteristics and qualities which are examples for others to follow."

"Ya Ummi, it is said that people had great respect and honour for your family even before Islam. So, is it true that even before your marriage, you were related to the Prophet ﷺ through your family?"

"Yes, my son, two of my elder sisters were married to the uncles of the Prophet ﷺ . So, my family was blessed with being linked to the Prophet ﷺ through my sisters' marriages. There is no doubt that God has favoured us; my mother is the envy of all women. She had such noble sons-in-law."

"Ya Ummi, I recognise that for each person, you keep referring to their relationship with the Prophet ﷺ , because essentially this is the link which gives them significance and honour. However, with regards to yourself, how did your relationship with the Prophet ﷺ start? In which circumstance was this bond formed, and where did your marriage take place?"

"O my Son, there is truth in the saying that marriages are made in heaven as the real beginning of this relationship is formed before we come into this world. This is by God's Will. As for the circumstances, I remember it was in the sixth year after Hijrah that the Prophet ﷺ came with fourteen hundred people to perform umrah.

However, they were refused entry. Following negotiations, a treaty was formed. It was agreed that the Muslims could not complete their umrah that year, but they could return the following year. The Prophet ﷺ returned the following year with two thousand Companions to complete the umrah. After completing the umrah, he camped in Mina.

I was thirty-nine years old at that time and had already been married twice. I was living with my sister in the house of Abbas. Both were concerned about my marriage. I had many proposals, but I had refused them all. It was in Mina that I first saw the Prophet ﷺ. Only God knows what my heart felt at that moment when my eyes first caught a glimpse of him. In that intense moment, I declared, 'I and the camel I am riding, I offer to the Prophet ﷺ.' When the people heard what I had said, they were shocked. However, my Lord verified my words' sanctity, and a Qur'anic verse was revealed in my favour. God blessed my marriage through Divine revelation. Upon my sister's request, Abbas approached the Prophet ﷺ and spoke about my proposal. The Prophet ﷺ did not hesitate and accepted the offer. Arrangements were then made for our wedding in Makkah. However, the Quraysh insisted that the Muslims leave Makkah as the three-day period had ended. The Prophet ﷺ explained what had occurred and offered them an invitation to the wedding. Despite this, they refused to allow us to perform the marriage in Makkah. So, the Prophet ﷺ kept to the agreement and left with his Companions. They camped at a place called Sarif, about ten kilometres out of Makkah, and it was there that our marriage was performed.

My parents had named me Barrah, which means a righteous woman; the Prophet ﷺ granted me a better name; Maymunah, which means 'full of blessings'. After the marriage, I accompanied the Prophet ﷺ back to Madinah, where I was made welcome by the other Mothers of the Faithful. I was only with the Prophet ﷺ for four years before he passed away. However, they were the best years of my life."

"Ya Ummi, even today when young people go into the presence of an awliya. The first questions they ask is whether one is married. It seems to be a major part of faith. Is it that important?"

"O my Son, the first mention of the word zawj (partner) in the Qur'an is in Surah Al-Baqarah where God said, 'O Adam, live with your wife in Paradise...' (2:35). As Adam was alone in paradise, he wished for a companion. So while he slept, God created Hawa. When he awoke, he saw and desired to be with Hawa, but God told him that this was not permissible unless he married her. Before that, he must pay a dowry. Adam did not know what this meant, so an angel was sent to instruct him that he should read salawat upon the Prophet ﷺ three times and that this would be considered the dowry.

So, the act of marriage is as old as humanity, as even the first human being could not find peace and comfort in paradise without a partner and was therefore married. It is not only the Sunnah of our father Adam and our mother Hawa but one of the greatest and beloved Sunnahs of the Prophet ﷺ .

O my son, I remember once, three men came to our household asking about the Prophet's ﷺ regular practices. We informed them about some of his routines. They were very disheartened to realise that they could never measure up to what the Prophet ﷺ could do. So, one of them promised to remain in prayer every night. The second pledged that he would fast every day continuously without taking a break. The third decided that he would never get married, which would become a distraction and an obstacle to his worship.

Eventually, when they met with the Prophet ﷺ , they were asked if they were the ones who had made these pledges. The Prophet ﷺ then said to them, 'By God, I am more submissive to God and fear Him more than you. Despite this, I fast, and then I break my fast. I pray, and I also rest, and I marry women. He who does not follow my Sunnah is not from me.'

There is no doubt that the Prophet ﷺ is the best and perfect example, as he showed us how best to maintain a balance in life. However, it is deeply saddening to see that today people calculate the benefits and losses of actions such as marriage in their minds. They fail to realise that their understanding is limited. In comparison, every *action and every blessed Sunnah of the Prophet* ﷺ *holds immense benefits, great virtues and hidden secrets. It is simple: if you want to follow his Sunnah, then God will make things easy for you.*

Aishah narrated that she heard the Prophet ﷺ say, 'When a bondsman marries, he completes half of his Din and that he should fear God for the remaining half.' This shows how important marriage is. God says in the Holy Qur'an, 'O you who believe, fear God, as He should be feared, and let not yourself die save as Muslims.' (3:102). The scholars explain that the verse indicates that you should not die unless you are married.

"Ya Ummi, clearly marriage is essential, but there must be a greater purpose which goes beyond this physical relationship. What is the wisdom behind this bond?"

"O my Son, you are asking about secrets when you struggle to even understand and act upon what is apparent. People think that they will lose their freedom by getting married, yet they fail to realise marriage's importance. If only they were to adhere to living their lives following the blessed Sunnah of the Prophet ﷺ, they would realise the real benefits of marriage. You should be grateful for your husbands and wives, as it is they that are saving you from hellfire. Otherwise, there are enough temptations for you to be committing obscene acts and sinning every day. Indeed, your partners are a great source of protection for you.

God describes this relationship in the Qur'an that you are a garment for them, and they are a garment for you. A garment provides cover, comfort, and protection. The Prophet ﷺ once said, 'O young people, whoever of you has the means should marry because this keeps the gaze lowered and is a protection for your private area. If you are unable to marry, then keep fasts because that will reduce your lust.'

In Surah Yasin, God says, 'Glory to God, Who created in pairs all things that the earth produces, as well as their own (human) kind and (other) things of which they have no knowledge.' (36:36). So, every living thing, whether humans, animals or plants, are created in pairs. This is what zawj means, to be a couple, and its purpose is to continue human beings and other living things. Through this relationship, which God has permitted, we fulfil this obligation and attain His pleasure. So my son, marriage is unquestionably one of the most beneficial Sunnahs. However, you have reduced marriage to a ceremony where everyone is invited apart from God and His Beloved."

"Ya Ummi, I am thinking about the awliya who do not need this relationship as they have surpassed such physical desires. They do not observe marriage because of the physical gratification; instead, they follow this Sunnah intending to maintain the practice of the Prophet ﷺ. So, when even the great awliya of this ummah follow and uphold such traditions, it leads to reason that this deed has to have a much greater purpose."

"The Prophet ﷺ never did anything which did not increase his desire to be with God, and which did not bring him closer to the Divine presence. In marriage, the Prophet n was being humble before his Lord. God Almighty placed great responsibilities on him, and he fulfilled every duty to the best of his ability.

O my Son, know that it is through marriage that God has allowed you to achieve nearness to Him. There is an instinct within you to seek companionship. What you seek is union with your Lord. However, as that is not possible, God has created a means for you to seek and achieve intimacy with someone in life. This way, you come to appreciate the joy and pleasure of this bond. Thus, the level of closeness and affection you hold in your marriage with your partner reflects divine intimacy.

Suppose you take care of this marriage and succeed in this temporal relationship. God will grant you a greater and everlasting union in the Hereafter. In this manner, a successful marriage prepares and helps you to accomplish intimacy with your Lord. If you find someone on this earth who may have many faults, but you overlook them, and still achieve a complete union; only then can you have a union with the One who is perfect.

As wives of the Prophet ﷺ, we were all blessed to succeed in our marriage. We were *able to refine noble characteristics through his love and guidance. O my son, it is through marriage and the tests and responsibilities that this brings which allow you to develop patience, mercy, compassion, steadfastness and many other good qualities."*

"Ya Ummi, you explain that marriage allows us to become better people by developing good manners and characteristics, but how can we decide what to look for in a wife or husband? Mawlana Shaykh Nazim says that some people are like waste bins, as they collect filth and rubbish. How can we see who is full of waste and who is not?"

"O my Son, the Prophet ﷺ said, "Three people have the right to God's help. The slave who tries to buy his freedom. The person who seeks to remain chaste by getting married. The one fighting in the cause of God.

It is true what your shaykh is saying. God Almighty has granted you such a great honour of being from humankind. Nevertheless, so many of you disgrace yourselves by abusing your bodies. From the beginning of creation, certain qualities have always been considered honourable in every society. Keeping yourself chaste and pure has always been regarded as a noble and moral virtue by all cultures and religions. Humanity has always been united in upholding the significance of marriage. They have celebrated this relationship through ceremonies, rituals, and customs. Since God has permitted this relationship only through matrimony, it has been sanctified, bringing endless mercy and blessings.

However, I see that in recent times this has changed because of your negligence. As your shaykh said, people have become like bins, collecting waste from here and there, saying they are exploring their freedom and possibilities. I am disappointed that you have become heedless in this manner. As you move away from the traditional ways, you have become accustomed to immorality. You are not even looking for these qualities in your partners. Instead, you mock and frown upon them, thinking that they are old fashioned. However, you must seek companionship in those that uphold noble qualities and characteristics.

O my son, the Prophet ﷺ once said, "You should marry women who are virgins, as they have sweet mouths, pure wombs and are easily pleased." He has indicated the qualities that you should look for in your partners. These attract Divine mercy and blessings, which then help make the marriage successful and prosperous."

"Ya Ummi, Mawlana Shaykh Nazim said about his wife: "She looks as pretty to me as the day I married her." Even after so many years, is it possible to maintain this level of love and affection between each other?"

"O my Son, this is possible as the love between them does not decrease with age because it is not based on lust. When you desire a woman, you will love and praise her, but once you have had your satisfaction, she will no longer look like a princess, and you will no longer be a prince. Within twenty days, all your passion diminishes. However, suppose this relationship is based on love and nurtured through selfless actions, care, and consideration. In that case, it continues to grow and blossoms over time.

God has indicated how this stability in marriage can be achieved. He uses the word 'Ma'ruf', which means kindness, by saying to men, 'Live with them on a footing of kindness and equity.' (4:19). Therefore, you should treat your wives with kindness and gentleness, as this will inspire softness in them and create a deeper affection and love for you. Your conduct with them will reflect on their behaviour towards you. You should realise that your wives have left their parents' home, where they were brought up with great care and love. If you treat them with harshness after marriage, it will cause them to be constantly reminded of their time with their own families. Then their hearts will yearn for their parents' love and will grow cold towards you.

O my son, in the last period of his life, the Prophet ﷺ had nine wives, but not one of us ever complained that we were upset and wanted to return to our parents' homes. This is how beautifully the Prophet ﷺ treated us. We did not want to leave the Prophet ﷺ for anything. I remember when God revealed the verse of Surah Al-

Ahzab in which we were given a choice, "O Prophet! Say to your wives: If you desire the life of this world and its glitter. Then come! I will make a provision for you and set you free in a handsome manner (divorce)." (33:28). We all cried so much upon hearing this and fell at the Prophet's ﷺ feet, seeking forgiveness for even the basic demands that we made. We all said that we did not wish for anything and we did not ever want to lose him. Even all the wealth in this world was no substitute for his companionship, and we could not imagine a life without him. Indeed, we all felt this way because of how the Prophet ﷺ treated us.

Aishah told me that once the Prophet ﷺ was resting his head in her lap. There was a full moon that night. She asked the Prophet ﷺ if anyone had as many good deeds as the stars in the sky. The Prophet ﷺ told her that it was Umar Ibn Al-Khattab. Upon hearing this, she was silent, and so the Prophet ﷺ asked her to continue. Aishah said she was expecting to hear that her father had that many good deeds. The Prophet ﷺ said, "O Humayrah, do you compare Umar with Abu Bakr? All of Umar's good deeds put together do not equal one deed of Abu Bakr." Aishah said that her face lit up, and she was pleased beyond words. This is how the Prophet ﷺ showed affection and consideration for us. He was always very affectionate and mindful of how we felt. Even his simplest action was full of kindness. It was in these simple things that our hearts were conquered, and our love for him has no bounds."

"Ya Ummi, such marriages seem rare where both partners are emotionally compatible and can sustain such consideration and appreciation for each other over time. How can we overcome our weaknesses and aspire to adopt such good characteristics?"

"O my son, indeed there are specific characteristics which God has naturally placed in all human beings. That is why features such as boldness and bravery, determination and strength are associated with men. You see traits such as love and tenderness, care and gentleness, compassion, and sacrifice in women. These qualities are revealed according to the way you face each situation. I am happy that even today, I see goodness in many ladies. They show great compassion and concern

for their families. It is their natural ability to be tolerant and merciful.

I remember that the Prophet ﷺ once explained that women are created from the rib, which is very delicate. If too much pressure is applied in attempting to straighten it, it will break. However, if left as it is, then it will always remain crooked. Suppose you are forceful and intimidate your wife in every situation; this will be very harmful and lead to separation and divorce. On the other hand, if you are a henpecked husband who has no say in any situation and is without authority, this is equally harmful. The Prophet ﷺ dislikes extremes, where the husband is weak and where the wife is harsh.

O my son, there is a good and bad side to each person. You should always focus on the goodness of people. Those who constantly emphasise others' weaknesses drive the other person away, creating a rift that draws more grief and despair in relationships. Such misery does not end with this life but can even carry on into the Hereafter. The Prophet ﷺ said that a woman could take three people to hell: her father, brother, and husband.

On the other hand, I also remember the Prophet ﷺ saying that the world is but a relish, and the best relish of this world is a pious woman. God has created all types of provisions for you, from food and clothes to health and wealth, but the most beneficial amongst them is indeed a pious wife. It is a pious woman that can change a disobedient husband into a God-fearing person and bring up her children with fine morals and good principles. She can resolve great disputes within families and have the wisdom to avert trouble and harm by uniting her household.

However, sometimes a wife can be so occupied with religious practices that she begins to neglect her husband's duties. This can also create coldness between her and those in her household. It is important that she be mindful of her obligations at home and not even keep a voluntary fast without her husband's permission.

O my son, I see that these days everyone is always demanding their rights. The Prophet ﷺ told us, "Know that you have a right over women, and they have a right over you." Undeniably, this is a two-way process, and each partner must be considerate of the others' needs. Your wife has a right over you. You must treat her well in matters of food and clothing. You also have a right over her; that she safeguards herself and the household. I agree that it may be difficult for you to find an ideal husband or wife and be mindful of all these rights in this relationship. Still, marriage is all about achieving a balance. Although there may be something in your partner which you dislike, at the same time, surely, there will be something you do like."

"Ya Ummi, it seems that in Islam, there is always a greater emphasis on women to be considerate of the rights of their husbands. Whereas with men, the focus is on worship, jihad, knowledge, and spirituality. Why do any of these elements not take precedence for women?"

"O my Son, there is great Divine wisdom behind the role of women. People think that women have a subordinate role in Islam, but this cannot be further from the truth. It is through the Prophet's ﷺ teachings that the status of women has been elevated. Don't you know that women were considered to have no soul? On the contrary, Islam has made it far easier for women to reach Divine acceptance and pleasure by heeding their natural characteristics. God has made it easy for women to attain high ranks through simple actions, which have great worth in His sight.

O my son, many examples can be told. The greatness of women is in their obedience to their husbands. Every woman can reach this position in the Divine presence by simply fulfilling her role as a wife. You can see how God graces obedient wives with His favours and mercy. However, be warned that just as this relationship brings about great benefits, it can equally draw God's anger. Indeed, both Nuh and Lut's wife invited the wrath of God through disobedience towards their husbands.

These days it has become common for women to talk ill of their husbands. The consequence of such conduct is that it causes bitterness between couples. The Prophet ﷺ said: "Whenever a woman steps out of her house with intent to *complain about her husband. She incurs the wrath of God and His angels.*" To have unrealistic expectations of the husband is what breeds ungratefulness. Her appreciation will have an impact on her husband as he, too, will value her. In this manner, love and harmony will increase in their household. Her righteous characteristics will be imprinted on her children."

"Ya Ummi, after the Prophet ﷺ passed away, sometime later you returned to Makkah for Hajj. You were taken seriously ill during this time, but you wanted to die outside of Makkah. Had you stayed in Makkah, you would have been buried in Al-Ma'la cemetery. Did you not prefer to be buried in Al-Ma'la or be taken to Al-Baqi' in Madinah?"

"On my third Hajj, my health deteriorated. I realised that these were my final days. The Prophet ﷺ had already told me that I would not die in Makkah. I knew the truth of his words. So I asked to be taken out of the city. I spent my final moments in the same place where my marriage with the Prophet ﷺ took place. My nephew, Abdullah Ibn Abbas, led my funeral, and since then, many travellers have come to my grave. I am grateful to my Lord, who has granted me this honour in life and death. Indeed, all these blessings are granted only because of my relationship and marriage with the Prophet ﷺ ."

"Ya Ummi, it is a blessing for those that get the opportunity to visit Khadijah and then to visit you as they leave for Madinah. We can only imagine how this must please the Prophet ﷺ . We hope that you pray for us at the time of our death and the grave, so we can stand as true servants before the Prophet ﷺ on the Day of Judgement."

"There is nothing like marriage, for two who love one another."

The Prophet Muhammad ﷺ

CONCLUSION

Being in harmony with what God has instructed, is the core of the Islamic faith. This is the pre-requisite for every believer in God. Throughout existence, societies have handed down traditions from generation to generation, however in Islam, the Sunnah is the perfect guidebook for all of mankind. The Prophet ﷺ said:

> *"None of you truly believes until his desires are in accordance*
> *with the very thing I have brought."*

The nineteen pious individuals in this volume are amongst the vast number of extraordinary people to have possessed real faith. God Almighty has never left a community or era throughout history without such saints. After the Prophetic Sunnah, these are the people whose lives, though seemingly mundane, are emblematic of what ours should emulate. Their purpose is to be of service to God's creation; and in doing so, they fulfil God's command on earth.

From negating the self – *"nobody, son of nobody"* – to adorning the cape of servanthood and remaining steadfast in their roles, they all share a common trait which places God at the centre of their existence. This is particularly noteworthy in our world where none other than God is at the summit of people's concerns.

Although these saints reach greatness due to their diligence in the *Din* (religion), they never want greatness for themselves. By seizing every opportunity before them, all they want is the chance to do good for others and be close to God. Mostly through strenuous spiritual practices and enduring debilitating afflictions, these saints become ennobled through determination and Divine Grace.

On account of this volume being introductory, my aim remains to make these people's lives accessible to people who know little or nothing about them. Although those mentioned in this volume are from a previous generation, the elasticity of their actions and life-altering lessons do not diminish with time. They inspire onlookers, seekers, wanderers, the lost and believers today to remember all of creation's need of God.

Plentitude in scarcity; Richness in poverty

When the Prophet ﷺ said, *"Poverty is my pride"* he was referring to our need of God, and how man is poor before the Majesty and Munificence of God. Realising this poverty and dependence on God is how man achieves proximity to Him. These *Generous Souls* are governed by this belief and by associating with them, we too have the opportunity to attain it and reap its ultimate reward – God's pleasure.

Each of these saints associated with someone whose noble link to God transformed their lives. There are numerous other examples of this throughout Islamic history, such as the Companions of the Prophet ﷺ or the dog that accompanied the Companions of the Cave. The moral here is that sanctity is achieved through association with those who associated with the beloveds of God – the *Generous Souls*.

If we look for them, with an internalised absolute need for God, they will be revealed to us. Should we be fortunate in that step, the duty then is to remain in their shadows for our salvation in both worlds.

So when glancing at the lives of these Generous Souls, remember to pay heed to their purpose, characteristics and way of life; for there are rare fruits in each of them.

Remember, even when fruit trees appear dead, they never really die; they just turn into a different form and are actually teeming with life. Their utility in any state, means that they are always emitting goodness.

Praise be to God, Lord of all Dominion. Excellent is He, from whom all strength and power is obtained. In Him do we trust. May God's blessings and peace be upon our master Muhammad ﷺ, and upon his family and Companions.